No Longer Bound

To: Ana, Bless you.

[signature]

3-21-15

No Longer Bound

My Voice My Freedom

Airyka Edwards

AuthorHouse™
1663 Liberty Drive
Bloomington, IN 47403
www.authorhouse.com
Phone: 1-800-839-8640

© 2015 Airyka Edwards. All rights reserved.

No part of this book may be reproduced, stored in a retrieval system, or
transmitted by any means without the written permission of the author.

No Content in this Book is intended to discredit Religion
of any kind, nor any Person of any Race.

Published by AuthorHouse 12/26/2014

ISBN: 978-1-4969-5858-7 (sc)
ISBN: 978-1-4969-5859-4 (hc)
ISBN: 978-1-4969-5864-8 (e)

Library of Congress Control Number: 2014922257

Any people depicted in stock imagery provided by Thinkstock are models,
and such images are being used for illustrative purposes only.
Certain stock imagery © Thinkstock.

This book is printed on acid-free paper.

Because of the dynamic nature of the Internet, any web addresses or links contained
in this book may have changed since publication and may no longer be valid. The views
expressed in this work are solely those of the author and do not necessarily reflect the
views of the publisher, and the publisher hereby disclaims any responsibility for them.

Scripture quotations marked KJV are from the Holy Bible, King James Version
(Authorized Version). First published in 1611. Quoted from the KJV Classic
Reference Bible, Copyright © 1983 by The Zondervan Corporation.

Contents

Dedication vii

Reviews ix

What People Are Saying! ix

Acknowledgements and Special Thanks........................ xiii

Words of Encouragement..xv

Acronyms.. xvii

Simple Introduction xix

Chapter One: My Birth 1

Chapter Two: My History...3

Chapter Three: From Home To Home............................8

Chapter Four: The Good My Mom Did 18

Chapter Five: My Life In Texas 22

Chapter Six: My Life With Tony................................... 32

Chapter Seven: When I Said I Do 47

Chapter Eight: Germany...54

Chapter Nine: Louisiana – Part I 67

Chapter Ten: Our Tour to Louisiana—Part II................ 81

Chapter Eleven: Our Transition To "Missouri" 93

Chapter Twelve: My Angels.. 124

Chapter Thirteen: Our Transition To

        "Missouri" Part II 148

Chapter Fourteen: My Purpose 154

Dedication

I'd now like to humbly thank my husband, Brett for giving me twenty plus years of your life. You are my true soul mate, my friend and my biggest supporter. I know people believed that we wouldn't make it, because we were from totally different backgrounds and yet, we have so much in common. Sweetheart you still intrigue me! You make life interesting every day. Thank you for the patience through the years that no one else could have had with me. Thank you for being my tranquility, my peacefulness when life gave me a rough ride. Thanks for drying my tears when I needed you most. Thanks for taking my children and treating them as your own all these years. Thank you for all the sacrifices you've made for our family and for me. Through all of our ups and downs you still……..and now I want you to know, honey I still……..Love you…..

Reviews

What People Are Saying!

Airyka Edwards No Longer Bound shares her own modern day Horatio Alger climb of rags to middle class riches and respectability. Born into a family with multiple siblings and too many fathers, her childhood was filled with hunger, cold and neglect instead of the warmth, love, and true affection every child needs and craves. Instead, like so many young women in inattentive families, she had to fight to preserve her own virtue as well as her physical and emotional survival.

In unflinching detail and at times painful specifics, Airyka Edwards tells of her childhood, her adolescent years and her early years as a young single mother. She also writes of her struggles as a military wife and her triumph as a faithful Christian woman, following the time-tested mandates of her Savior. Her narrative more often than not, reads like a delightfully charming, friendly visit over coffee with a girlfriend. She makes it clear that her primary purpose in writing such a personal story is to provide a warning to young girls about the many dangers out there and most of all, to share a you-can-make-it-too story of triumph. The most incredible part is the amazingly capable, beautiful and

Airyka Edwards

intelligent woman, who has not only survived but thrived beyond any logical expectations.

No Longer Bound should be put into the hands of all young people, struggling to make their way, trying to avoid the dangerous pitfalls while finding their own place in this very complicated world. Hers is an excellent example that says in America, you can still achieve your dreams, with faith and hard work, and that you are not bound to a life time of misery, no matter what station of life you are born to. As a black single mother in America, she could easily have fallen into the self-pity pit and yet, she never gave up, simply accepting a lesser fate. Refusing to succumb to drugs, teen pregnancy and the other many pitfalls of her humble beginnings, Airyka Edwards is today a successful mother, wife, and medical professional who defies all the statistics of her origins. No Longer Bound not only tells her personal story, it serves as an inspiration to any who struggle with adversity, past, present, or future, and how through faith in Jesus Christ, a fine life might be achieved, by any definition of the word, success.

Laura L. Valenti, author
The Heart of the spring,
The Heart of the Spring Lives On,
The Heart of the Spring Comes Home,
Between the Star and the Cross: The Choice and
Between the Star and the Cross: The Election
Ozark Meth: A Journey of Destruction and Deliverance with co-author Dick Dixon
www.BetweentheStarandtheCross.com

No Longer Bound

What an awesome, riveting read! We picked this book to begin reading it, and we didn't (couldn't) put it down until we had finished it. This was an exciting testimonial that witnessed the healing power of a merciful, loving God. It depicts a life with experience, wisdom and spiritual strength. It substantiates the fact that God has a master plan, and all of us fit neatly into it. We should never give up on our destiny and we should never allow anyone to count us out. Her willingness to share even the most intimate details of her life experiences, is a testament to her strength and determination to send a message to everyone, that no matter what the circumstances are, "Hold On" and watch God change things. A must read.

Pastor

This book is an easy read, but stirs all the emotions that one could possibly experience. The way the author expresses herself, you truly feel that you are present in the circumstance feeling the pain that she endured; and yet, there is always a theme of hope throughout her story that is revealed in her writing that supported by her faith. This is an inspiring story of one who rises from poverty to a comfortable life-style of peace and acceptance. I would definitely recommend this book for anyone who seems to be struggling with life. Well done!

Supervisor, Hospital Pastoral Services

Acknowledgements and Special Thanks

To thank God is simply an understatement, but all I can say is "THANK YOU JESUS", for all you have brought me through. "I still have a praise inside of me!" I'm so thankful that You, Lord, allowed me to accomplish this. Thank You for every laughter, every tear, every pain, and every failure, but most of all every success!

I would like to send a special thanks to my mother.

Thanks to (All) of my supportive coworkers; I love and appreciate each of you.

All the staff at Author House Publishing Co. that worked so diligently with me.

Thanks to my husband for the financial support to fund my dream, I know we needed a new roof on the house, (smile) but instead you allow me to publish.

"Thanks" to all of my Patients that have allowed me the privilege to care for you, we laugh together, we cry together; we pray together, most of all we heal together. For without each of you my life would be void. You are the reason I am happy to get up each day to take my daily journey, you make me smile! I sincerely

Airyka Edwards

thank God for the experience with each of you. I'm so grateful for the opportunity to serve you. I love you All!

Those of you whom I did not, rather could not mention, please take no offense. I cannot name everyone. God has blessed me with so many awesome people in my life and I am so grateful for each of you.

I would like to honor my dad; I know you are smiling in heaven waiting on me. I miss you so much! "I love you Daddy"

I would like to thank my Pastor and First Lady for their assistance with my Subtitles

Words of Encouragement

To all those who read this book, I hope and pray to embrace your hearts and minds. I may not be able to reach all of you, but if I can just help one or a few of you that have lost all hope. I pray that you gain and regain your inner strength, your dream and yourself worth. My prayer is that God gives you what you need through my words and my testimony so that one day I can hear your words and your testimony. Remember the root word of testimony is "TEST", so expect to go through and be tested and tried by God and by life lessons. If Daniel can survive the lion's den, just think of what God can bring you out of!

I would like to extend a huge thanks to all who chose to read this book.

Acronyms

Dear: My nickname given to me by Brett (my husband). Two weeks after we were married he called my place of employment and asked for "Rebecca", so they paged me over the intercom. I finally get to the phone and he'd hung up. I called the house and he answered saying, "I'm sorry, "Dear" it will never happen again." So for over twenty years I have been called "Dear". (Laugh)

PCS: A military transition to another duty station or assignment

B-K: African American

Y-T: Caucasian: when my children were younger I taught them not to stereotype people by the color of their skin. I told them to find another way to identify them; "the girl in the lace dress" or "the boy in the red shirt", but through the years without my knowledge they acquired their own language; B-K for Blacks or African American and Y-T for Caucasians. I thought it was too cute!

FRG -Family Readiness Group in military

IDF: Interdenomination (Church of the Living God)

All Bible Text Taken From:

BGW - Bible Gateway- King James Version-KJV-by Public Domain

Simple Introduction

I invite you, my readers, to come and take this journey with me. I'd like to share some of my life experiences, events, some of my memory triggers and how I was affected by it all. I want to engage you in my triumphs, fears, pain, shame and my anger, but most of all, my freedom. I would like to purge my mind into this book and namely bring you in to relive and share how you can regain your sanity, your freedom, and your own power from within. It's there; you simply haven't released it yet.

I started off not knowing if this would be a "Christian" book or just my autobiography, but as I began to think and write, I thought, "How can it not be a "Christian" book if you are a Christ like person; a "Christian" woman? So take it as you may, I must include my walk with God, my faith, and my failures with God also. As you read you will get to know me and just who I am and how God allowed me to heal and mend my life back together.

It's August 24, 2013, I think it's one of my sisters birthday....which one I'm not sure. It's been months now, close to a year since my desire surged to write my life story.

Chapter One

My Birth

This Is My Story

It was September 1963; fall had come early in a small town down in Mississippi when I was introduced to this world. Some say this cruel world, but I say not all cruel, but sometimes beautiful, wonderful and a fun world. Better yet... "the United States of America"! I was seven pounds at birth, a little frail, but alive. My mother took me home, "Don't know if my dad was there or not", most likely not. Don't gain a preconception of him as he is not what you think!

Weeks later I am back at the Memorial Hospital...diagnosis... malnutrition. I lost weight because I couldn't eat by mouth or drink. I was told by family an IV and feeding tubes were started in my foot, because I had no veins from being too dehydrated! Well, God apparently wanted me here He spared my life.

My dad told me years later he recalled the hospital "being in a very rural area" and they did not take very good care of me. My dad said he took me away from there. His words exactly, "Baby you would have died if I hadn't taken you somewhere else and I didn't want my child to die!"

I was born to one of the most beautiful women in Mississippi, Delores Brown and Amos Walker. My parents were not married. My mother is American Chickasaw Indian. I never knew my mother with two arms. My mother's fiancé was teaching her to drive when they had a horrible accident. My mother was hospitalized for four months after that. She was in a coma for three of those months, I'm told. She had a severed right arm which had to be amputated. Mom was alive by the grace of God and only nineteen or twenty years old. She has a scar on her left leg where she had fifty to sixty staples to hold that side of her leg together. She also has a scar on the side of her head from wounds that she received. My mother managed life with one arm. My dad was just an everyday average, hard working African American from Mississippi. They were both alcoholics.

I, myself, never thought I was beautiful…didn't inherit my mother's long beautiful black hair nor her beautiful, gorgeous, flawless skin or skin color. My sisters, four pretty ones, one all right and me, just "good personality", was always reminded that I was not the prettiest peach on the tree, skinny and bald headed. All the way to 2010 they still commented on my hair and how it made me look. They never thought of how their comments made me feel all those years, because I never let anyone know they got to me or hurt me in any way.

Be careful of the stones you throw. God's Word says, *"Be not forgetful to entertain strangers: for thereby some have entertained angels unawares." Hebrews 13:2 KJV*

Chapter Two

My History

Hope Lost And Found

I am from a family of fourteen children and twelve are still living. One child was lost as a result of a miscarriage my mother had. A second child, my brother Sammy passed away at six months old on a cold wintery night. He froze to death. My sister (who actually found him the next morning) I don't believe that she has ever really recovered from that event. I believe the only obituary we had about Sammy's funeral was a book marker with his name and a few words on it with the Lord's Prayer. If I'm not mistaken she still possesses that today. My sister was just a kid herself.

We never had heat or hot running water in our house. My mother said she was going to get some milk and didn't return home for days. The neighbors called the welfare people which were social services to come and take all of us away, as I remember back then, there weren't many places to put eight black children, instead God worked on our side. Social Workers worked hard to get heat and water turned on (no hot water heater) but still water. This was just another weekend shocker! Now still surviving are six girls and six boys. I am the ninth child, I believe of the twelve. Out of the boys, I know four of my brothers. One was adopted at a young age and the other one lived with his dad and their family. I have only seen him once when I was about ten years old. He came for a weekend visit to my real mom's house. He was in town from Las Vegas. As he approached the porch we ran into the house to tell our mother there was someone in the yard that looked like a white man, she went to the door and saw him, then said, "Oh, honey, that's ya'lls brother". Well, I was about to faint! There was something I apparently missed along the way! All I remember is he was a very handsome young man and had a beautiful kid with him named Shone, my nephew. We all had different fathers, except two siblings that had the same father we believe.

As I write this book, it has evoked so many memories. Years before I left to live with my dad and stepmom, I have some memories that triggers thoughts of my mom, other "stepdads", "uncles" and whomever else were there, drunk, falling over, fighting on the front porch, neighbors watching as my sister and I, along with some brothers would go down the hill to some other neighbors house. Sometimes we got to sleep in their house on the floor, sometimes they wouldn't answer, so we would find an abandoned car or truck and sleep in it.

I remember some nights we were so hungry and cold we'd go looking for my mom and step dad, "Mr. Blue." We would go to the local cafés and find them. They were drinking and partying all night. Often times four or five of us kids would go into "Ms. Tigers" or Tully's café and ask my mother and her men friends for money to eat. They were cross eyed and drunk so they would give us any money they had. They were so out of it they really knew

No Longer Bound

nothing that was going on around them. I still can smell the "corn whiskey" and "Schlitz beer."

I also remember once we went around the corner to Mrs. Emma's house. Her husband "CJ" was home that night and was intoxicated. She still tried to help us. I think there were five or six of us asking her if we could stay. She snuck us in her house under the bed in another room. Just as we tried to sleep, "CJ" began to beat her! We wanted to help so bad, but hungry and exhausted we just lay under the bed and slept. I remember crying silently. I just wanted to eat and sleep in peace for once. The next morning she woke us up and rushed us out of the house.

There were some nights; my mom would lie down as if she was going to stay home. I remember one particular night I got to lay with her in bed. I slept at the bottom of her bed. I recall holding on to her ankle in hopes that if she tried to leave I'd feel her move and wake up. Well, she left and I was tired and sound asleep. I remember it was about 2 A. M. and I jumped up looking for my mom and my siblings, but everyone was gone. They had all left the house and me alone. I screamed so loud and cried so hard. I was scared to death, so I ran outside still screaming, one of my brothers heard me and ran up the hill to get me. I recall hearing dogs howling that night. The rhapsodic of my fear was intense.

As I reminisce on the past, the pain is like yesterday. I recall days being very hungry not knowing where or how we'd eat. I remember Mr. "Casey" and Mrs. Ann Casey. They were the owners of the local café nearby. Often times they would save the scraps from their rush hour lunch and dinner and place them in a bag and send them to my mother by us. The scraps consisted of chicken "necks, backs, liver and gizzards". My mother would cook them up and serve with rice and butter if we had butter. The Casey's were good people. They really tried to help, often times it was difficult for them to run a business and give food away but yet still they did. I would work for them sometimes cleaning their house, help run their laundry mat and Mrs. Casey would pay me on weekends. Sometimes that was the highlight of my weekend just to work and earn a buck or two for food.

I also recall days my mother would have us selling "Grit" papers, for income, a newspaper magazine with advertisements in it. I believe it sold for about twenty five cents back then.

One day just hanging out playing at my mother's house we caught wind of some bad news. Word came out that a neighborhood friend of the family lost her little boy. "Johnny had died". Johnny, I think, was close to two years old. They said he had worms; all he ate was candy and sometimes dirt...yes I said dirt from outside, I know because we sometimes did the same thing. I didn't understand all that back then "worms"?? humm??

Today is February 2014. My sister's stepbrother passed away. I looked on the funeral home site to read his obituary but to no avail. I decided to search the internet on an archive site to see if I knew anyone. Oh, my...Little Johnny's name was mentioned in an obituary of a sibling that was several years old. I saw names of the family I knew back then in the 70's.

Surprise after surprise, I saw my first cousin's name "Ronnie". Well, no one had called to tell me my mom's nephew, my first cousin was deceased. Wow!!!! Shocker after shocker! I began to

No Longer Bound

go back just three years on the archive site and found maybe ten to fifteen people that I knew well. A day or so passed and my sister, Ranne called. I'd previously told her if her stepsister came to town for their brother's funeral to please let me speak to her, if she was still nice! Oh, bless God she was! My sister called and I spoke with Tammy she was our piano player in the Baptist church and a good one I might add! My goodness, talking with her the memories flooded in, as we continued talking of our childhood and our lives. We never thought our lives would ever cross like this again. The truth came out about twenty plus years ago that Ranne was a sibling to four other people on the other side of town.

It was somewhere around the early 1970's my mother and father really turned their life around. She joined church; "Missionary Baptist Church." Some of us kids were baptized there. I don't quite remember exactly when, I just know it was during a revival when the doors of the church were "open" and that was your time to stand up and accept the Lord as your "Personal Savior". This was the time when my mother met my youngest sister's father.

Chapter Three

From Home To Home

There's Always Hope

By now at age six years old, I went to live with my Dad and new stepmom on "Lyle Street" in Mississippi. My new stepmother never let me forget I had two left shoes on that didn't match. She said I had mange on my legs and feet. Years ago that was the old peoples way of describing how dirty you were. My new stepmom's grandson, Jacob also lived with us. He was not a true relative of mine, but I considered him my "stepbrother". He taunted me for years. I enjoyed having family, so I never told anyone.

My fondest memories are of my dad going and coming home from work, off the graveyard shift. He would always put his cap on my head and me on his knee. He would bounce me up and down like a bucking horse. That would only last about ten minutes, because he either had to go to work or bed. I remember when my dad would take me school shopping he would always make a point to go pick my other sister's up and take them shopping too. My dad always thought of others. Months and years would pass as I remember my dad every Friday coming home from work. He

8

would give my stepmom all of his check, but twenty dollars. He would say, "I'm going to get a haircut". Well, I knew I wouldn't see him until Sunday.

I recall a few times the cops would pick my dad up for being intoxicated. He parked on the side of a road or at a vacant parking lot. They'd just take him to the station, put him in a holding cell and leave the door open until he slept it off normally by Sunday morning. Sounds like an old western TV show, only thing was missing were the actors, because all of this that is written had real characters, real events and no actors.

Finally my step mom got tired after awhile on Sundays waiting on him inside the house, so she would wait on the porch. He usually came home around 6 P. M. When he returned she'd make us kids throw rocks at him. A few times she pulled the shot gun out! She was a true Hatfield!

One day he came home with a lady in the car, "Ms. Howard". My stepmom was asked by my dad to make her acquaintance with her. With all the grace and dignity she had, she shook hands with "Ms. Howards". She was very polite, asking where she was from and so on. I think my stepmom knew from that moment on she had lost my dad. She often took it out on me. Every morning she'd take my brother and me to the school we attended. She would turn around in her seat and ask, Duke, (that was my nick name) did you get your lunch"? As soon as I said "No Ma'am ", I'd get slapped across the face. I believe that was the first time I saw stars and Jesus all at the same time. Oh, well, I had a beautiful room, beautiful clothes and I had dolls, but I was not allowed to play with them or comb their hair. Loneliness filled my soul.

Airyka Edwards

Years passed and by now it was around 1975 or 76. I got to go live with my real mom and family again. I was sort of happy, but frightened. I didn't know what to expect. My family would take my money and make me clean the house. It was at this point I developed OCD. A disease called Obsessive Compulsive Disorder. My stepmother was a clean freak. I worked on weekends and summers in order to have new shoes and clothes to wear to school. Having a job allowed me to be able to buy my mother a Mother's Day and birthday gift, which I personally wanted to do. She would always say, "I wish you would have given me the money instead!"

A few weeks passed when my dad called to tell me my stepbrother, Jacob was dead! I was devastated. I didn't know how to grieve or cry. My heart was broken. Although he had been mean to me for years, he was still my family. Mom wouldn't let me go to the funeral services in fear that my stepmom would take me back. However she did allow my sister to walk with me to the Funeral Home which was about five miles away. Wow...very hard for a thirteen year old!

As I tried to adjust to life at my mom's, life just got harder and harder at times. I remember always having to either get a taxi to school or walk miles. For awhile my mother would make me go about a mile up the street every morning before school to get her a bag of tomatoes and a half pound cake or an angel food cake. I'd run all the way there and back to try to catch the bus, but I never made it. I was determined to get to school though. The harder I pushed to get to school each morning, my mother found more things for me to do.

No Longer Bound

One morning I remember making it to the bus stop. It was in the late 70's when Mini skirts and dresses were in. I had on a dress that was a "little short", but in style. This particular morning I paid my twenty cents to ride the bus and a young lady that got on the bus asked me to get up and move to another seat. I felt like "Rosa Parks". (Laugh) For once in my life I stood up for myself. I said, "Um, no I'm staying at this seat. I paid my twenty cents." She looked at me with all the evil that was in her and said, "You're gonna pay for that, watch your back." I was a little scared, because that young lady and her family was well known as "bullies" and would back up what they said. So the very next morning off to the bus stop again. As soon as I proceeded to get in line to await the bus, out of nowhere, here comes "Odessa"! That was her name. She pushed me once and to the ground I went. I recall her beating my tail like I was her child! My goodness, she tore my little "afro puff" hair piece off and she bit me on my left cheek! She was like a raging bull! I had to go back home. I was bleeding pretty badly, so I thought. Think I saw "stars and Jesus" again. (Laugh)

Every first of the month, I had to walk about a mile and a half with mom to get our food stamp allotment, after which we would go to Pack n Save to get groceries. I had to push two baskets full of food which were extremely heavy, (remember my mother only had one arm). Mom would either call for a taxi or we'd stand outside of the store hoping someone would offer to take us home. She would pay them with an uncooked "fryer chicken" she'd bought, because she had no money left. Three days later the welfare check would come and she would once again keep me home from school. We would go to town. She would buy herself

Airyka Edwards

a new dress and shoes every month. I would get treated to lunch at "Wally's", next door to "Ed's Dollar Store".

By this time one of my sister's was age fourteen and pregnant. She was able to receive "WIC" products. God forbid that we missed those nine months to pick up six cans of juice, two gallons of milk, cheese, beans, and powdered eggs!

I recall on a very cold rainy day mother kept me home again. She said, "Let's go get the WIC items". I said, "But Mom, it's raining and how will we get home with it?" She said, "Just start walking, gal!" So I did! Needless to say I had to carry the box with six cans of juice and two gallons of milk in the rain. The rain was so bad it hurt my face. I cried all the way home with sore arms and nappy hair.

By now I was in the seventh grade at school and mom starts to get sick a lot with pleurisy. Well, who gets to stay at home with her for a month, "yours truly"! It was the month of April, I remember, because the first week of May after food stamps and welfare day, she told me to get dressed, get out of there and go to school. I said, "Mom, why? Its finals and I haven't been there." She said, "I don't care. Get out!" So I did, sobbing my eyes out. Of course, everyone in school was asking, "So where have you been?" I actually caught up with my school work (but not math) believe it or not, but had to go to summer school. Back then it cost thirty dollars per class and taxi fees as no bus ran during the summer. Wouldn't you know mom was on a diet now, so no more pound cakes! I failed seventh grade math. Math was my challenge and you had to pass that class. I finished summer school by July 15th. I started to get little odd jobs which allowed me to

No Longer Bound

buy school clothes and have lunch money. My dad retired and I started getting a check from social security or should I say, "My mother started getting a check".

Let's jump a bit, while in the eighth grade, the next school year I was being followed daily and I didn't know why. One day while walking home from school approaching a corner I would come upon a dead spot where a person could no longer see me. From behind I was jumped by a guy. He threw me to the ground and stared at me with a death look and said, "I could kill you". I said, "Do it". He jumped up and ran. I was terrified, scared to death and shaking when I got home. I just set on the porch to calm down. After several times of incidents like this within a year's time I finally told my mom. She told my dad. He said, "If I catch him I'll kill him, ain't nobody gonna mess with my daughter!" One day I was late coming home from school, because I took another route home. I was trying to avoid passing by the Funeral Home. I hated and still hate passing funeral homes. My mom was concerned and was standing on the porch waiting for me as I walked as fast as I could up the hill to our house. The same guy came running down the hill and my mom yelled, "Don't you touch my child!" Oh my, for a moment I felt she cared about me!

The torture went on for a solid year. Days, months, and years went by and I never saw him again. After this another event took place. I would take taxis to school some mornings. One particular driver would always seem to give my mother and I a ride from the store whenever I called for a taxi. One day instead of taking me home from work at "Lonnie's Truck Stop", "yes thirteen and working", the driver took me out Highway 61 on a long dark road. He told me I either do what he says or "I die!" I stated, "You're gonna have to

Airyka Edwards

kill me today". At this point I'm tired of being bullied, but scared out of my mind. He pulled a knife out and I said these words, "Put me out of my misery." He said a few choice words, touched me a few unwanted places and drove me home. I wasn't brave, I was horrified! "There are angels among us!"

I have never had a birthday party. Once my mother said I could have a few girls over and they could actually come in the house; although I was too ashamed to let them in. I asked three girls and one came, "my friend Ellen Prater." I had a small pound cake I'd spread icing on and we had cherry cool aide. We were sitting on my mother's bed and spilled a "sip" of my cool aide. I was in so much trouble my mother made me take the bedspread down to the washateria, so that ended that party.

Things were so intense for me. I started to lose a lot of weight that I didn't have to lose. My mother noticed at times I wasn't eating and I slept a lot. So many days I was the only one who would clean the house, wash all the dishes (for which I had to heat water on the stove), sweep the floors and took all the laundry down the hill to wash. All the pressure and responsibility weighed heavily, so my mother took me to the doctor. It was discovered I had a nerve problem and I had Anemia "an abnormal blood disorder "I was put on medication. I mentioned O.C.D. –Obsessive Compulsive Disorder; my mother tried to do the best she could, but the house was filthy. I had to do all of that just to lie down at night. On top of all of that our house was "infested" with critters; roaches, rats and God only knew what else came through the cracks and crannies! Sometimes I wished that we lived in the projects. It was in the Subdivision. I thought all rich people lived there. Everyone had a brick home and hot water. I had no idea it was for people

No Longer Bound

with low income! Sad to say, but we thought they were better off than we were. I don't know if that was innocents or ignorance. A few of those rats I actually named (Laugh).

I remember writing to my uncle and aunt in Alabama begging them to send me a bus ticket to let me come live with them. I didn't ask my mother. Well, two weeks later my aunt Anna sent a money order for twenty-two dollars for a Greyhound bus ticket to Alabama. I packed a box of clothes and was sitting on the front porch when my mother got home from a doctor appointment. I said, "Mom, I'm moving to Alabama." She nicely informed me, "Over her dead body!" Well, that was the end of that!

Now it was summer again and fruit trees are blooming. We always ate fruit off of the neighbor's trees. I saw the plum trees at the Lancaster's house down the road and went over to ask Mrs. Lancaster if I may pick some plums. She readily stated, "Yes, sweetheart". So her husband, Mr. Lancaster offered to help me. She thought that was sweet of him. He asked me to hold the bag open as he placed plums in the bag. When he slowly put fruit in the Pack n Save bag he would reach over and touch my breast. I kept holding the bag so I could get more fruit until finally I said, "Thank you, Mr. Lancaster". He handed me a quarter and asked me not to tell Mrs. Lancaster. I never spoke of it until now.

We had some really good neighbors back then. I remember the family down the hill (dirt road), Mrs. Carrie, Mr. Isaiah, Vonnie Lee, Shelia Ann and Bonnie. They had a few boys Larry Joe and Jimmy Lee. Mrs. Carrie and my mom were pretty close. We all loved that family. They actually became my sister and my second

Airyka Edwards

home. That entire family was so kind to our family, but they were exceptionally kind to me.

One day I was down there just visiting and confided in Vonnie Lee about my sister's boyfriend (thirty-five) was touching me when I was about thirteen years old and he wanted to go further. I told her every detail, I needed to tell someone. However I didn't expect her to tell my sister. At first I was upset with her, but then I began to think, this was the only way she can protect me was by telling my sister. My sister confronted me about it and I told her the truth, but she still dated him. Shelia Ann was my rock. She would always ask about my day or how school was going. She'd let me set in her room for hours just talking. The day Shelia Ann told me she had a job in Illinois I felt like a truck hit me!

When Mrs. Carrie took sick I was asked to set with her after school and on weekends while the family worked. The day Mrs. Carrie passed away I remember my mother calling me at school, because she didn't want me to go by after school and face the shock. I remember the night of the viewing; the family set me on the front row with them. I was honored. I was so hurt she was gone. It was like losing a mom. I recall crying so bad towards the end the family and the funeral director ushered me out to another room. The other room had another body being held. Well, they had no idea; I started to cry harder, because I was scared to death! I was about to run and make another wall in that place! At that point I was done grieving! (Laugh)

Many times my mother would entertain men "carpenters", such as Mr. Bo, who was going to fix some part of the house. Truly we were never allowed in the presence of adults. We could not

No Longer Bound

even walk through the same room, but on certain occasions Mom would say "Duke come say "hi" to Mr. Whomever was there at the time. I would be offered to set on the couch and chat. I had a feeling what was going to be next. Yes, touching, yes Mom sitting right over in her chair as though she didn't see a thing. I would say, "Well, Mr. so & so, it was nice to see you" and make up an excuse to go outside. It sounds like my mom wasn't a good person. She really was, but had no guidance. Her parents died when she was very young. She soon married, so she had to live, learn, and earn her mistakes, but through all those dark times there were some good times too. And through all of that, I chose (not) to be a bitter person.

My message to all girls, teens, ladies, and gents; "protect your children, especially your daughters. Look, listen, observe, conserve, and preserve them."

No matter what happened I've always respected and obeyed my mother. Yes she was supposed to protect and shelter me from bad things such as being molested so many times. Instead sometimes I felt as though I paid the price for the roof getting fixed or whatever needed to be done. God still brought me out alright! I wouldn't change one moment. I believe those experiences made me who I am today!

We should still "Honor thy father and thy mother that thy days may be long upon the land, which the Lord thy God giveth thee" Exodus 20:12 KJV

Chapter Four

The Good My Mom Did

Getting Saved

For the most part, my mother always instilled in us God and church. Mom had strong faith in God and always made us get up on Sundays and go to church. We had to attend Sunday school even if no church was going on. We were Baptist for a few years until one day, my brother; Everett came home from college and talked to my mother about being saved. We thought we were saved, but we were in for a big surprise. One day my brother pulled me aside to speak with me alone. He knew I wanted and needed more. My brother talked to me for about eight hours that day. He showed me passages in the Bible and introduced me to "good music". We're talking about "Shirley Caesar" (which is my all time favorite), "Walter Hawkins", "Andrae Crouch", and the list goes on! He tried talking to my other sisters. They always had an excuse or no time, but they were listening to "The Commodores", "Gladys Knight & The Pips", "The OJay's" and so on. I absorbed all I could. I was thirsty for something more than what I had. My brother prayed with me and he soon had to leave to go back to college in Ohio. My mother truly thought my brother was crazy.

18

No Longer Bound

When he left, she called my uncle in Michigan he was a Pentecostal preacher. It wasn't two days after my mother spoke with my uncle when he arrived at our house at 2:30 A.M.! He said, "Delores, my sister, I'm here to take you and the kids to Tarry!" Oh goodness, I was terrified! What in the world is Tarry? I soon found out down in a tiny town in Mississippi at a little church no bigger than a one bedroom house. My uncle, the preacher from the other church, and his wife made us stand up in front of the altar with our hands up in the air. They would come by and slap our hands with theirs. I thought, "Oh my goodness, they are going to rape and shoot us with our hands up!" They also spoke other languages, which I know now as "tongues". We had an exhausting night! On top of all that I didn't get the "Holy Ghost", but I sure was scared and mad at my brother by now for even talking to my mother.

A couple weeks later my uncle located a church for us to attend. It was good bye Baptist and hello "crazies"! (Aka Pentecostals)

A few weeks passed and Mom said I "had to get saved", "Me" out of everyone! It was on a Sunday night we had other church guests from the First Apostolic Pentecostal Church. There was quite a few Y-T's in attendance. They were singing their hearts out, shouting, clapping and dancing like "crazies". Suddenly my mother grabbed my hand and said go to the altar, the spirit is moving! Oh goodness, I just wanted out, but little did she know I was fully prepared for this! I asked a little cute sister next to me, "Sis Irene, (RIP)", I said, "So how do you speak in tongues?" She said, "Sis Airyka, God has to speak through you." Well, I needed to speak something fast! My mother said "Get saved or don't come home with me tonight", so I started jumping around like the rest of the "crazies". Then I started stomping with high heeled stacked

Airyka Edwards

shoes on and a long light blue maxi dress. Suddenly something hit me and it wasn't Jesus. Baby, let me tell you I clowned like I never had before, started hissing like a snake, and started cursing saying the s... word. By now I'm drooling and foaming at the mouth. If you know anything about Pentecostals from the old days, "the more you drool the better", so I mastered it all that night! It's a wonder God didn't strike me down right then. By now I'm tired after all that jumping, screaming, foaming, and kicking poor Brother Travis in his precious jewels with those "stacked heels". So I calmed down, fell on the floor and started saying, "Jesus, Jesus, Jesus". I heard the saints say, "Satan is gone. Jesus is in the house!" I wanted to yell, "No, He ain't, i'm just tired!" Oh, Bless God!! My mother came back up to the altar after I came to my senses and said, "Pastor, what must I do if she does that at home?" He said, "Sister Delores, start praying and call me." I said to myself, "Ya'll don't have to worry about that again! That was too much work to fake!" Needless to say I didn't get saved that night. So remember "faking and shaking" can't help you to make it!

The next Sunday I thought I'd give it all a break. The Pastor was preaching and said something about being baptized "in the name of Jesus". I figured I had been dunked once in the Baptist church, what the heck, a second time ain't gonna hurt! Apparently the first time didn't work or I wouldn't have been perpetrating! Long story short, I got baptized in the name of Jesus, filled with the Holy Ghost, and begged for the fire (and that with fire)!

My sister saw a change in me and asked what's wrong? What did I do? I said, "Liz, I got saved and baptized in Jesus name and I really

No Longer Bound

want to go to heaven." I also told her I loved our new church "The Church of the Deliverance". The rest is history!

People it does not matter, what denomination, what title you carry, we are all praising the same God trying to get to the same heaven. God is coming back for his Bride not a title or Denomination So I ask for forgiveness now if I offend the Baptist or the Pentecostal. No harm taken, just trying to get a point across. If David in the Bible could dance, well, honey, so can I! I love to shout and Praise God! I'm thankful today for my mother answering the call and making that decision. I appreciate my uncle that has since passed away (RIP) Uncle "HW" Herman B. Well, God sent!

Chapter Five

My Life In Texas

It's A New Day

It was approaching the summer of 1979, one of my sisters had married and moved to Texas while another moved to California. My mom got a call from both sisters asking for me to come help them. They were both pregnant and each had another child already to care for. She agreed to let me go. She said, "Make a choice." I chose Texas! I had been there previously with a church choir group and knew that weekend; Texas was going to be my way out and my new home!

Where do I begin? Let's try from the beginning June 15, 1979 I arrived in Texas! At that time I was so excited to be a part of my sister's life and her family. By the time I arrived she was a few months from delivery. September approached and my niece was born.

I was really enjoying the church there and had started to date. At age fifteen years old with the assurance that we "are all saved", "sanctified", and "Holy Ghost filled", I had no worries of anyone touching me inappropriately. Well girl, wake up and smell the carnations, because I guess saved people have feelings, needs, and lustful thoughts too! I guess that is why the Bible speaks of adultery and fornication! ... {For if they cannot contain, let them marry, *for it is better to marry than to burn*. 1 Corinthians 7:9} well, some of those brothers and sisters must have been on fire, because here we go to the rodeo honey!

I was so happy at this point to fellowship with the new saints that I'd met. Everyone seemed to be on top of their game. I loved what I saw so far. The day after arriving to Texas the church chartered a minibus to Little Rock, Arkansas to one of the church council meetings. I was invited to sing with the state choir. Wow... all this was just awesome! I was taking it all in. That night when the main service took place I remember praising God like I'd never praised before. I felt freedom! Finally! I worshipped and when the spirit kept moving, the shouting started and I was right there in the middle of it all, shouting for the first time under the real anointing this time. I had never seen God move in such a powerful way, nor had I been in the midst of so many people allowing God to use them in such a way.

As time moved on, we, (my sister, brother-in-law, niece, nephew and I) attended church twice on Sundays, Tuesday nights was Bible study, Wednesday nights was Joy night and Thursday nights was choir rehearsal Friday night regular church night. I'm worn out just talking about it (Laugh), but I enjoyed every minute and every service. My soul and inner being was longing for the fulfilling of a huge void. Remember the more we eat the more we want. The more money we make the more we want. The more we buy the more we "see" that we want to buy. There is always a void in our lives. Sometimes we don't realize it until the void becomes apparent. Then we listen to ourselves and decide we're not happy. We are really just content most of the time, but not happy.

"I believe that there is no true happiness on this earth." Material things have us in a joyous mood for a time, but when the new wears off there goes the joy. The only true happiness is God and God Himself in us; that is the only true happiness that exists.

By now the summer was over and it was time for me to return home to Mississippi. I had prayed and prayed that God would speak to my mother and let me stay in Texas. My mother refused and told me to come back home the next weekend. I thought to myself, God, you were going to bless my stay here forever; at least for a few years? My heart was breaking. I dreaded even the very thought of returning to that hell God had gotten me out of. I asked my sister to please speak with our mom to let me stay in Texas. Mom continuously said, "No, I want my child home." So I asked the pastor to talk with my mom. The answer was still "no".........I sat and cried for days. I could not and would not return back to Mississippi! So I made a deal with my mom. I said, "Mom, you can have all of my social security check if you let me stay." She paused, and then said," Well how will you get money?" I said," Mom, I'll work for it, just please let me stay." So she did. I sincerely appreciate my sister to this day for rescuing me.

I soon found out Texas was a little different than Mississippi. You couldn't work at fifteen or sixteen years old there; you had to be eighteen. So I went to school and did some babysitting on the side. Once again I found myself needing a ride to school. Some of the teens from church attended the same High School as I did. Just about every morning I was late; the last one to walk into the classroom at 8:15 to 8:30 a.m. How embarrassing! At this time my sister walked to work not far from the apartment where we lived. My brother-in-law was in the military, so he took the car each morning. Someone around the corner would walk my niece and nephew to the sitter.

As time went on my sister and brother-in-law were always fighting verbally and sometimes it got pretty heated!. I would either try to stop them or leave the house, telling myself, "This too shall pass. Just get through the day, girl get through the day."

I really started to miss my mother and needed a mom; as now I was sixteen. I would call her occasionally. She would tell the operator when I called collect to disconnect our conversation after two minutes. That's all my mother would talk to me was two minutes! I asked her a couple times to send me a few dollars and she stated if I was going to start that just come home.

Soon I turned eighteen! I landed a job at a factory, "Furniture Manufactory." I worked there for five years. I made lead woman and finally department supervisor. The pay wasn't bad either. Well, let's back up a bit. I had dropped out of school in my sophomore year. Later I started night adult classes. I had to hitch rides there and back also. Just in case you haven't noticed, I was determined! Some nights I had no ride home at 9 P.M., so I'd take off walking. The school wasn't in the best neighborhood either, but I walked, and God kept me.

I remember going home one weekend to visit my mom and dad. I remember the taxi driver on the way from the bus station. I gave my mother's address; he looked in the review mirror saying

Airyka Edwards

I know where you live and who you are with a smirk on his face "You're one of the Brown girls, Delores's daughter. He stated yes, she sure had some good looking daughters. I felt molested once again just by his eyes that day. I felt low and disgusted! I had saved some money after turning eighteen and working, so I wanted to bless my mother and show her how prosperous I was. I took six hundred dollars cash home with me that weekend to take my mother shopping. We went several places in the mall. I bought her a nice watch and ring she picked out and a beautiful housecoat, belt with bling bling on it, shoes and dress from Towers Department store. I went a little over my budget. I still had to get back home to Texas on the Greyhound bus. I had just enough left over for my ticket minus seven dollars I came up short on. I remember I asked my mother if she could spot me the seven dollars to purchase the ticket back. Her response was, "I guess all my children are just poverty like." Oh my goodness how "grimace" that made me feel! Needless to say she did not give me the money. My little sister, Ranne called me in the other room to give me the money out of money I had brought to her. That made me feel so bereaved to have to take anything back of what I had given her, but I had to get back to Texas and boy I couldn't wait! I did mail the money back to her with interest.

By now my sister and brother-in-law were really having problems, so I befriended a sister in the church whose husband had gone to Korea with the military. She invited me to spend the night a few times and I happily accepted. We became good friends. Our friendship would have its rough spots through the years, but for the most part she helped me through a very tough time. She was a young wife with a child. She fed me, clothed me, and gave

No Longer Bound

me extra money sometimes for personal needs. Robin was an awesome friend!

Months went by Robin worked daily and I babysat for her. A year had passed and her husband returned home. Our pastor told me I should move out and let them have their privacy. I wanted to, but I had nowhere to go. I asked Robin if she would let me stay for one month. I landed a job at Big Boy's, waitressing on the night shift. That lasted about two days. I called the church one night for someone to come pick me up. A trucker had pinched me on the posterior and I was highly offended. I told the manager and he simply said, "That's how you get tips!" Well, I had a tip for him. I quit that night after making the call. The pastor himself came to get me. He took me home to Robin's house. He came into the house and sat down on the couch. He invited me to set down with him, but on his lap. Well, that was the beginning of hell starting over again. My feelings were so hurt. I was so disappointed in the man I thought so highly of. I admired his faith in God and he had the nerve to make his moves on me! I felt as though I had been tasered! I recall the dark pain devouring me for days, weeks and went into months of disbelief. It was like I'd been trapped for years in a prison in Mississippi. No one really knew until I confided in my sister. Then you make a run for it and you actually think you're safe! Then comes another big disappointment! You were never safe. You simply had a short break."

I remember one day just walking out of church and I kept walking down the street. I wept and wept that day, but never questioned God, "Why?" I just kept repeating "Ok, girl, this too shall pass. This too shall pass. This too shall pass." Finally I talked myself in going back to church, but not being able to focus and praise that much.

Airyka Edwards

A few months later I was tested for my G.E.D. and wouldn't you know a man named "Math" came to see me......I failed that part! I had to do what they called remediation until I got it! Bless the Lord, finally! Almost a year later I tested for my G.E.D. and passed! I had never been so proud of myself! First achievement to success is "Education!" I had another sibling to do the same thing some twenty years later acquiring her G.E.D. Today she has an associate's degree. She had some of that determination in her too!

As time went on I got my own place with another sister in the church. She was a divorcee with three kids who came to stay with her. We roomed together for about six months. One day she stated that I ate a piece of meat intended for her kids. I felt awful, so I borrowed twenty dollars from someone at church and replaced the whole package, although I had eaten only a very small piece. I didn't know her kids were coming over or that they would be staying the weekend. Some months later I moved out.

For several years I had moved in and out with roommates. Either there were no funds for them to pay neither rent nor utilities, or they got married. During all this time so much was going on. People were getting married left and right or they were leaving the church for some reason or another. I also was hearing the pastor had been with several sisters married and unmarried. It was not all hearsay. I personally witnessed encounters that had gone on for years. I personally experienced him, touching me and asking for favors. I made the decision to take care of my ailing father and weeks later I was exiled from the church. It really hurt to be treated in such a way after giving just about all you have and sacrificing to give to the church. I was about twenty four years old

No Longer Bound

at the time. I recall once we had what was called a "Big Bill Wave." The pastor asked everyone to give one thousand dollars and those who couldn't to give five hundred dollars, no less. He gave us one month to gather our funds. Wow! I went out and got a second job at a Pizza place. I worked there giving every tip and every paycheck; even added from my check from Furniture Factory where I worked full time. I wanted to have my one thousand dollars when time came. I also saw people obtain loans they could not afford. People let their cars go back to the dealers just to get their money. Some homes were lost. So many sacrifices were made, but finally a month later it was about forty members that had their one thousand dollars and twenty members came up with their five hundred dollars. Music started playing. We rallied around the church praising God for the money to "purchase land" for our new church that was to be built. Needless to say no land as far as I know was ever purchased. I know for sure no new facility was built. A few weeks and months to follow one Wednesday night was a business meeting at the church. I went. The floor was open for question. I simply asked "What happened to the money for our new church?" (By now the church water was turned off because the bill wasn't paid.) Well, the pastor's wife hushed me up quickly and took me outside asking me why would I disrespect pastor like that and ask such a question?

"Note to self".....If you give your hard earned monies I believe you should have the right to know where it goes; just my opinion. Now, trust me when I say this, "I believe we all gave from our hearts believing God told our pastor to have us do this, so we did what we "thought" God said. I "now" still believe if you give with a happy heart, not expecting a "favor" from the Lord, you will be

29

Airyka Edwards

blessed. I myself, feel as though I am still riding on the blessings of giving abundantly. I gave back then with a pure heart as I do today. My mother always told us, "The hand that gives gathers." If you simply open your hand and hearts to give before you have closed your hands God has already blessed you. It may not always be with money. It could be healing, a home, your freedom or simply a closer walk with Him.

I remember when people were hungry always hoping some church member would invite them over for dinner. I recall once a family with two small children, husband and wife along with about seven brothers of the church were living in a one room, one bath hotel room, because none of them had a place to live. They all worked and I didn't understand back then for the life of my why seven people couldn't get together and rent an apartment or house for that matter. Well, I would hate to guess that all of their monies were going to the church. I believe, God's will is for us is "*that thou mayest prosper and be in health, even as thy soul prospereth.*" 3 John: 1: 2

Something was wrong here. We were not prospering, but shortly after all that the pastor got a new house, new car, purchased a time share and took a trip to Mexico and a few other places. I personally can't and won't say that's where our money went, because I have no proof. Now, you the readers are going, "What, do you mean you have no proof?" Well, I wasn't there to see nor have I ever seen the church records. The records were never shared or discussed with the members as far as I know, in the eight years I attended there. I rarely missed, maybe only once or twice in that time period. For the record "my personal" lawyer told me I can write anything I choose as long as "I know its truth."

No Longer Bound

So what may seem obvious I cannot say for sure. All I can say is that I never saw or have seen a new church facility to this day. But I truly thank God for the experience He gave me and allowed me to have with some of the saints of God and the fellowship I had. I was taught to give from my heart, but that church didn't teach me that. God gave me the spirit of giving from a very young age.

A Year later I called the pastor's wife and she met me at the park. I told her of all or most of what happened to me concerning her husband, "The Pastor." She listened, asked me two or three questions and said, "Thanks." She then asked me, "Why now, why tell me now?" I stated, "Because my life has been hell and I wanted you to know it's because of him. Now I can move on." We departed and never spoke of that conversation again. My life was so complicated at that time; Mind you I have also done things I'm not proud of either.

If you noticed, I did not name, names. That was not my purpose to expose. My purpose was to inform Pastors, Bishops, leaders, Sisters and Brothers to please be mindful when you make the decision to cross the line out of God's will, you embark on another's future. The pleasure for a moment will leave a lifetime impression. Yes, I'm scarred for life, but scars will and can heal. God's mercy endures forever with me. Be blessed...Be healed!

Remember this; should we choose to step out of God's will, there are steep consequences. I paid dearly; let's continue our journey to my next chapter.

Remember "*For God is not the author of confusion, but of peace*" 1 Corinthians 14:33

Chapter Six

My Life With Tony

Escaping the Flames

It was August 1987: I was introduced to the man who would steal my heart, my true virginity, and my innocence. In early August I was so frustrated and pretty much put out of the church choir. I was no longer allowed to teach Sunday school or participate in any functions of the church. A month prior, in July, I received a call from my dad's doctor and my mother stating Dad was sick and needed me to come home. I am my father's only child. I spoke with the pastor and told him what was going on. He nicely told me I could not go home to take care of my father unless I gave a certain amount of money to the church. I had less than what I was told to give. I needed every penny I had to get home on a Greyhound bus and for eating while there in Mississippi to take care of my dad. I disobeyed the pastor's orders and went home to be with the only man who had ever taken care of me.

I started to think I needed to get some type of experience in taking care of my dad. I remember him asking me to pass him a urinal and I just cried. He said, "Its okay baby I'll get it." I was

No Longer Bound

young and didn't really know anything. I prayed and asked God to help me, teach me and give me the courage to make it through all this. I never wanted to become a nurse aide because I felt that was just too much for me to handle, but I seriously have a respect for nurse aides. I wanted to be around older people to observe and learn from them. I did just that without doing hands on. We never had grandparents because by the time we were all born our grandparents had passed away.

When I returned to Texas, I met Mr. Tony, smooth talking and somewhat handsome. In my family we breed like rabbits, so within weeks the rest was history.

I will be totally honest with you. I felt I had made a horrible choice in allowing myself "an unwed woman" to get pregnant! I was doing an internship at "channel 8" in Texas Monday through Thursday and free on Fridays. I would shadow the reporters for sixteen hours per day. This was during my transition to "My Life with Tony". I started to feel sick some mornings not realizing there was a possibility I could be pregnant!

When I did find out that I was, I spoke to Tony about an abortion. I told him I wasn't ready for a child in my life. I was about to pursue my dream of going to school for journalism.

Since I never had to work on Friday I scheduled an appointment to have an abortion. The station then asked me to work that day so I rescheduled my appointment for the next Friday, in the meantime, praying and asking God for guidance. Again the station called asking me to help them out. When this routine happened a third time, I gave Tony the three hundred dollars back and looked

Airyka Edwards

towards heaven and said, "Okay Lord, I get it. I can't go through with this and you spoke loud and clear; no abortion for me!"

By December 1987, I got my first real side of Tony when he gave me fifty dollars to go buy a Christmas tree. I wasn't told not to spend the whole fifty dollars, so when he asked me for the change I gave him three dollars and some cents. Out of nowhere, I got slapped across my face! I think I saw "stars and Jesus" all at the same time again! That was the beginning of my long three years with him. My message here, "Don't ever allow a man to do that to you; not even once!"

As time moved on my son, my sweet little blessing entered this world. Weeks later I ventured out looking for a job. I found it very hard for me to leave my child, but I had to. I remember one day while interviewing for a position, I took my son with me, the supervisor asked, "Honey, are you going to be able to let someone care for him while you work?" I said, "Yes, ma'am, I have to, I need the job." I landed a job at Tender Loving Care Center as a housekeeper. My dream for journalism faded.

A year or so passed and as the beatings came more frequent, I would pack and leave. At one point I moved all the way to Florida with a friend for two months. I got a job, trying to start a new life. I decided to call Tony one night and he talked me into coming back. I did because after all, he was the father of my child. He did well for a few months and then there were more beatings. This time I said I'm leaving for good, called a friend and moved to Georgia. I stayed there for a few months and got a job. My friend's husband was in the military and wanted to take me out to eat and job hunting. One day while driving me around, he wanted to take

34

No Longer Bound

me to a hotel instead. I remember saying I was on my cycle for that month and I cried so bad he took me back to the house. I'd been friends with this family for years, admired their marriage, and now discovered it was all a "Big facade". Having so many let downs and disappointments in my life, it wasn't funny, but my favorite saying through all of it was, "this too shall pass."

Once again, Tony talked me into coming back home and this time I was happy to get away from the Georgia situation. About a month later I became pregnant with my daughter. I was disappointed to be pregnant, but happy it was going to be a girl. My thoughts were, my goodness, I can barely take care of one kid, moving in and out! Now I need to really think of stability.

I made up my mind I was going to marry Tony. We were going to have two children together and I really wanted my children to have a "Mother and Father" family. Tony had asked me many times if I would marry him. I always made excuses when in fact I was scared because he was already abusive. We discussed getting married before we had our daughter and he was happy I even entertained the thought. The next week he kept telling me there was something he needed to tell me. I repeatedly asked, what is it you need to tell me? He said, "But you'll just leave me again if I tell you the truth." My thoughts were "my goodness, I'm with a murderer or something!" Well the next day while he was at work the mail came and it was to Mr. and "Mrs." Tony A. I knew I wasn't a "Mrs." yet so I proceeded to open the mail. Wow! What a shocker I was in for! Mr. and Mrs. Tony A. needed to file taxes for the year prior! What! File taxes together! My mind is racing going "you can only file together if you're married to each other!" Yes, well that was the little something he failed to tell me weeks

35

Airyka Edwards

before or how about when we met! I'd made the statement one day to him in our earlier dating days, "There's no future with a married man and so I'd never date one." He claimed that's why he never told me he was still married, but "separated" for three years and had never filed for divorce.

I knew up front what I was getting! Don't assume anything! I assumed Tony was single. After all he approached me, not I, him! It doesn't matter who approached whom. Do your homework; I did a background check on my next serious man! (Laugh)

I remember one stormy day a year prior, while going to sign up for housing assistance there was a huge waiting list, so I was stuck for at least a year. I worked up until two days before the birth of Addison, my daughter. I recall my blood pressure was so high; they were trying to give me medicine. The last I remembered I was going into convulsions. Crazy, but after all that, I just laid there on oxygen thinking, "God, please let my blood pressure go down. I have to get my tubes tied tomorrow." Thank God, I was a perfect score the next day for surgery! I remember waking up from surgery asking for a Wendy's burger!

As the days followed, I was pressured by Tony to get back to work, so two weeks later I was back at work. My blood pressure sky rocketed and a week later, one of my co-workers had to rush me to the ER; 180/110. My goodness, I don't think I'd ever seen numbers like that!

It wasn't enough I'd had two hard pregnancies, vomiting from morning sickness, evening sickness and simply just being alive sickness, that went on with each pregnancy for seven months.

36

No Longer Bound

I was barely one hundred pounds soaking when I got pregnant. After the second pregnancy, it was easy to just do what was normal for me to regurgitate. Finally two months before delivery with each child I could eat a meal, but only at night. Tony always did the cooking. I gained seventy seven pounds in two months! That was ten pounds a week. The doctor at each appointment was happy until three to four weeks later I was continuing to gain. So at the time of delivery I weighed a whopping one hundred seventy seven pounds. I lost it all in three months after delivery watching "Joan Lunden" on her morning show with her new born exercising and walking a lot.

It was approximately three weeks after that, I came home from work one day with a headache, from God knows where. My blood pressure was up again, but I had two children and had to keep going. That Saturday I came home about 3:45 P. M. and lay on the couch. Tony proceeded to say, "Here, get the kids. I'm tired; I've had them all day!" I asked him, "Please just give me thirty minutes to get rid of this headache." He said, "No." He was leaving to go out. I stated, "Do whatever, I'll be fine." He said, "What does that mean, you're leaving me again?" I said, "Maybe and this time I will get child support". My goodness, that statement got me a beating like I'd never had. He yanked me off the couch and punched my head against the hallway wall about twenty times. I lost count. I remember my son, who was two years of age getting a vase and trying to help me by hitting his father. My daughter was barely three weeks old. I remember Tony chocking me until I passed out. When I came to he was gone and my son was over me crying. I called a friend I worked with years before to please come get me and my babies and she did. I vowed that day my children would

37

never be around nor hear violence as long as they were with me, ever again! My friend, Sherrie allowed me to stay with her for awhile until I got situated. A few weeks later I remembered a year before I had signed up for the housing assistance, so I went to check on it over in Cheyenne County. The Lady awarded me with a certificate for a two bedroom place. Oh my goodness......I was thrilled until she told me I had to pay the deposit and get the lights turned on. I thought, ok, I have no money. With the only check I'd gotten since on my own I'd been buying Pampers, paying daycare and giving my friend gas money to help her some. She never asked me for anything. Once again Sherrie came through for me and obtained a loan in her name to get my deposit and lights turned on. I had to pay two hundred dollars for my lights, because I had forgotten a few years before I allowed my sister to use my name for her utilities. Although I had no idea how all that worked, but I know no one would pay the last bill so I could get my lights on; except Sherrie. I thanked God for her every day, even now! I can truly say it does pay to treat people right and never burn your bridges or bite the hand that feeds you. *"The Lord is my shepherd; I shall not want."* Psalms 23: 1.

As my children and I settled in we had nothing to move except our clothes. Everything at Tony's was his except my daughter's crib. I applied for food assistance and got it about seven days later. But what was I to do until then? I had pride and didn't want to ask people for money or food, Sherrie had done enough. I called my sister and asked if she could just bring some Ramen Noodles for my son to eat. She came about eight hours later. I was so thankful. My child had stated hours before something no mother wants to hear, "Mommy, I'm hungry." My heart sank. As time went on I received my food assistance. I filled my cabinets and refrigerator and have never been low again on food.

I bonded with my children, spending as much time as I could with them when I wasn't working my second job. I also taught them to love each other no matter what. From the time they learned to walk and talk I enforced love and support for the other.

It was starting to get cold by November or December 1990 and I felt it every day, pushing my daughter in the stroller to work and my son walking next to me. I had them bundled up the best I could. The next week my daughter got so sick. I took her in to the doctor to find she had pneumonia. I was horrified. I felt like a bad parent allowing this to happen to my five month old child. God healed her and the doctors from Prince Women's Hospital in Texas took very good care of her.

God really blessed us in the following days, weeks and months. My co-workers, on their days off would take my children and babysit them while I worked so I didn't have to pay childcare. Everyone in my department took a rotation in babysitting on their day off. I never had to pay any of them. Finally I got daycare for them free and I received a promotion on my job; assistant housekeeping and laundry supervisor. I was thrilled! Six months later I made Supervisor/ Director, had my photo taken in a suit and given a gold plated name tag. Sounds crazy, huh? Name tag, but when it is earned, you're really happy. I still have in my possession the gold plated name tag! I was on the Wall of Fame with the other directors. Then six months later, I was asked to be on the admissions team, "The A Team", because I was awesome

Airyka Edwards

at customer service and loved to talk with the resident's. Their families loved me. I'd found my calling!

A couple years later I managed to reach my goal of purchasing my own home. Wow, I remember going to look at the place. It was sham racked on the inside from people living there prior to moving out. But I had a vision! I took my sister over to look at this place with me. She and my brother-in-law thought I was insane. *"Now faith is the substance of things hoped for, the evidence of things not seen." Hebrews 11:1 KJV* I kept telling them I had a wonderful vision of this place, "You'll see!" That was right after Christmas 1992.

I did receive one child support check before Tony moved to Washington and no more from then on. I would periodically call and ask if he would send something to help with child care and their expenses. I wasted a phone call each time. I did however give his name to the food stamp assistance people. I don't understand why most girls and women refuse to give the father's name when asked, while applying for assistance. Case workers always ask on the form who is the father or mother for that matter, of your child? and a way to contact. I don't get it! While he or she is out enjoying life with someone else making more babies, somehow you find yourself not wanting to get him or her in any trouble for neglecting "their" responsibilities to the child. Remember it is not charity. Your child deserves decent clothes and shoes even if the father or mother has to pay a price. "It takes two" as the old saying goes.

I remember writing a letter to the housing authority in Cheyenne County, informing them that I'd made Director at the nursing home where I worked. I was making better money and no longer needed the assistance. I asked to be taken off of housing. I remember taking the letter to them in person. The sweet little lady said, "Sweetheart you don't have to do this. Most girls keep it as long as they can." I smiled and told the lady, "I kept it as long as I needed." She continued reading the letter because I thought it needed to be in writing for me to be removed from assistance. The lady looked up once more and said, "Honey I'm proud of you." That was my first step from "Poverty to Paradise!"

I put five hundred dollars of my tax money down on my house and got a lawyer to look at my contract. He did it for free; he saw I was trying to better myself. By the end of January 1993 I had keys in my hand. It was a job and a half getting my house together. I had been collecting pictures and things that I had found for five or ten dollars on sale to decorate my new home. I got to work and within two and a half weeks after cleaning, putting up curtains and pictures, my children and I, spent our first night in our home. I was receiving fifty dollars in food stamps at the time. I was able to fill my cabinets with twenty to thirty can goods and ten packages of meat until my next pay check. I would buy ten packages every two weeks to keep meat and vegetables. My kids were thrilled. People were so kind to me back then. My friend, Larry, from the nursing home where I worked, came over and did some miscellaneous repairs for me. Another person gave me a color television for which I picked up the payments. Larry gave me a dresser and lamps discontinued from the nursing home. My co-workers at the Nursing Home gave me a house warming party at my home during lunch one day. I was so blessed and so grateful! Things were looking up and at that same time I had been dating

Airyka Edwards

this good looking cowboy for about a year. His good looks were all he had going for him. He was a cheater and a half. God gave me the courage one day to say, goodbye to him. I gained a really good friend from that relationship "his sister, Mae Bell." I was on my own, but happy.

By summer, the children and I were going to the lake. We loved to drive out there and have breakfast on a blanket. The children would play in the water. By ten or eleven we'd go home and spend the remainder of the day together. Some weekends we would just take off and drive to Benton or San Antonio to the flea markets or to whatever we wanted to do.

Life was good until I started crying all the time and didn't know why. I thought. "God, what is going on?" I have been blessed with a good job. I'm a director at the nursing home; I love my job, my staff and co-workers. I've purchased my first home. My children are healthy and happy. What is wrong? I continued to ask myself. As I was having a conversation about a month later with the social worker at the nursing home, she began telling me things she was going through. I said, "But you are married and have a wonderful husband and children." She was in the same boat as I. Depression had hit us both. I did some research in my family to find out that depression waved through our family like a rushing river! very strong in our blood line. I had to deal and fight once again. I was already fighting a demon…Bulimia, absolutely no one knew about. "Another personal hell" I held on to for fifteen years.

I want to elaborate more on Anorexia and Bulimia for girls, boy's teens and adults that may suffer from this disease.

42

Anorexia nervosa: is a serious eating disorder that affects women and men of all ages; it can damage your health and even threaten your life: other factors with Anorexia: Refusal to maintain a healthy body weight, an intense fear of gaining weight, a distorted body image.

Bulimia nervosa: is an eating disorder characterized by frequent episodes of binge eating, followed by frantic efforts to avoid gaining weight. It affects women and men of all ages.

Definition text obtained from online "Helpguide.Org"

We "you" put your bodies and lives at risk for low potassium levels, irregular heartbeat, lethargic, ulcers, weakness, dizziness and so many other health issues.

I know this disease by first name. I know its voice when it calls my name and no matter how young or old you are you answer it most of the time. It is "always" in the back of your mind. There are good treatments for this disease, but you have to be absolutely sure you can and will "accept" the treatment plans. I am fifty years of age probably fifty-one by the time my book is published and everyday is a constant struggle for me with Bulimia.

I have had all the symptoms including hair loss, lack of calcium in your body especially your teeth. I have dealt with this demon most of my life. I cannot tell you how many times I have sat down for lunch or dinner either with family or a friend and excused myself from the table with the "lame excuse", "Oh my goodness something was wrong with "my food". I feel sick." It works every

43

Airyka Edwards

time. The person you are with shows empathy when you return and you have done it again without blinking an eye.

I used to live on a bag of lemons and sour pickles. They would shrink my stomach so I could virtually go days sometimes weeks without eating food. I have triggers to this day. I refuse to even get pickles on a burger or with any food. I literally shake when cutting lemons at home to go in our ice tea. I have been caught by my husband eating a lemon after cutting some. I would put salt on it and devour it as if it was a chocolate cake. Remember my "nervous stomach, "nerve pills?" Well I'd developed ulcers at that time also a very common symptom of the disease.

Remember- laxatives, vomiting, diuretics or enemas, even excessive exercising are "all" forms of "Bulimia." There is a Hugh difference between being healthy and being ill. This is mostly induced mentally, which is mind boggling when you think about it. You even feel guilt and ashamed that you allow yourself to eat so, "you" will put your finger down your throat and induce vomiting. If a woman or man already thinks that she or he is unattractive that most likely is low self esteem, then you are at "high risk." Remember body image is not all we are made of it is just a portion. The real beauty is within.

All I have mentioned is simply a negative way to cope with what's going on in the inside, when truly we have created this monster on the outside. I'm saying if you were an alcoholic you will always be an alcoholic. It doesn't mean you still drink every day, but it is a characteristic that you are always one drink away from reoccurrence or history repeating itself.

44

Once Bulimic and Anorexic always Bulimic and Anorexic, but we learn to deal, fight and sustain each day. I say it isn't any worse than any other addiction because it can kill you just like drugs. It hurts your family to see you like that just like drugs or alcohol do. If you drink and drive, you risk having an accident. If you are weak and lethargic from not eating for days, you could also have an accident while driving.

Is it any worse than any other type of addiction? My opinion we are all in the same class -"addicts". However Anorexia is more like a terminal Cancer, once it has you it's almost impossible to cure.

"And they overcame him by the blood of the lamb and by the word of their testimony Revelations 12:1............" In order to have a testimony we must go through test in our lives. "The will of God will not take you where the grace of God will not protect you."

I finally went to see a doctor to get help. He gave me medication for my depression. I took the medication as directed for a few months and as time went on I gradually weaned myself off of it. I hate taking medications. I never took my first Asprin for a headache until I was thirty years old. I finally overcame the demon known as depression. It was very difficult. Some days were harder than others. I remember being in the car with my sister taking her to see a lawyer to file for divorce, which she never completed. We laughed so hard that day, reminiscing about the past. The minute she exited the vehicle, I balled my eyes out! Luckily, I had sunglasses. By the time my sister came back out, my eyes were almost swollen shut. But as my favorite saying goes "This too shall pass" and it did!

Airyka Edwards

God saw me through all of my pain and successes once again. Always have a dream, a vision, something to look forward to. I'd walked threw a few rough patches of leaves and bumped a few trees on the way, but God delivered me from the depression. I was blessed once again to get up on my feet. It's called "survival mode".

Time went on; I was enjoying life and starting to go out on the town a bit.

Chapter Seven

When I Said I Do

It was January 1994 when I met the man I would marry. We dated for eleven months. He was very nice, soft spoken and broke. I was comfortable but lonely. My children's father and I had been apart for three years at the time. He had moved on and was living in Washington State, where he passed away from heart disease. I dated some before meeting Brett. One guy was "the cowboy" who had me from hello in those wrangles, but he turned out to be a cheater. Another guy I dated was nice, quiet but not for me. He was an orderly at the nursing home where I worked and he turned out to be one of my stalkers. After that I stopped dating and just threw myself into my children and my work.

In December 1993 my staff at the nursing home wanted all of us to go out and have some "real fun", as they put it. Of all places they wanted to go two stepping! I was like "really girls?" I got my sister to babysit for me and off we went. My assistants and I went to eat Mexican food before we went to Denim and Diamonds County Western Club. I guess the food didn't set well with Ms. Shantell because she stayed in the bathroom most of the time while I was asked to dance all night. Finally around 1 A.M. the place

Airyka Edwards

was closing and Shantell was most certainly ready to go home! I'd collected about ten little pieces of paper with phone numbers. I pitched every one of them. I simply wanted a nice night out and I ended up having a blast!

A few weeks later a guy calls me and tried to make me remember who he was. I didn't recall ever giving my phone number out. I had two babies to raise, but my friend had slipped my number to the man who is now my husband. I do remember being really mean to him. He would come over a few times to sit with my friend and I at the dance club. I would make him get up. I said, "Honey, you can't sit here because the cowboys won't ask us to dance", and they were lined up to dance with me. So he politely moved. A few weeks later my girlfriend and I met him out again, and lo and behold he tried to sit with me again and again. I nicely said," You can't sit here, because the cowboys will think I'm with you and won't ask me to dance." So he moved again. I was a mess!

He called me another day and wanted to take me out to eat. He said, "Away from the club scene." I enjoyed the dancing at the club scene, but I did accept his invitation to my favorite Chinese Restaurant and we had an awesome time. He ate, I picked, and we talked and laughed for hours. I loved his sense of humor and he loved mine. We both loved country music and loved to dance, so we hit it off pretty good. He was actually newly divorced, with three children involved. One day a few weeks later I had the urge to tell him to go back to his ex wife and give it a chance for the children's sake. After all I was a single mother and knew how hard it was for single parents. I told him I would wait, but if he wanted to stay with her I would totally respect him for that. He assured me he had tried all he was going to try and he was done. I was

48

really afraid of dating or marrying someone who was divorced. I thought I'm just asking for more trouble. I even made him mad one day on purpose to try and make him break it off with me. The man was in love! I thought by then I was too, but too scared to let go and love. I always thought of my babies. I had to make the right decision for them. They'd never met anyone I'd dated before. I didn't want to bring guys in and out of my children's lives unless it was going to be permanent.

One weekend Brett came to visit and stayed the weekend with me. It was the end of May. My children were gone for the summer to visit their grandmother in Louisiana. I got Brett's wallet and obtained his social security number. I called my cop friend to pull a favor for me and had him do a background check. "Know what you are getting and who you are getting." Remember everything that looks good "ain't of God". I had to make sure he was safe for my babies. I didn't want a child molester or drug addict around my children. Trust me I have seen people play it off until they said I do and then they wished they hadn't. I was determined to have a good guy and a good marriage. If I was going to do this, I wanted it done right.

By July Brett came down one Monday after work from Amarillo, Texas. He wanted to go out to eat at our favorite place, Wonhong Chinese Restaurant. I said, "No I don't want to go anywhere." I'd worked ten hours and I was very tired. So instead he said, "Let's go on a drive to our favorite spot by the lake." I agreed. It was there at Ben O'l Hollow Lake, he proposed to me and I said yes! We immediately got started on wedding plans and said our "I do's" on November 19, 1994.

Airyka Edwards

Some months before our wedding day, on numerous weekends my family would come over and borrow my car with a full tank of gas, then they would bring it back that night on empty. I always filled up my tank on paydays for two weeks to get from home, work, daycare or school for my children. There were times after buying my food for two weeks they'd come over and take a few packages of meat out of my freezer. They would also eat about all my lunchmeat and cheese that was my lunch for the upcoming weeks. I knew sometimes they just didn't have and they were hungry. I never said no to them. I never knew Brett really noticed all those weekends until a week before we got married he politely told me, "the free store" is coming to an end when we get married. He stated, "I've watched people take from you long enough and it's over." I kind of got a little offended because after all, that was my family. He looked at things, black and white. He said, "You work every day, even on call to provide for yourself and your children and you have never asked me for a dime." He said, "Sweetheart, they can do the same!" Well, he was right. He stated that his responsibility is to me and our children, no one else. I felt so protected by him and again I had to appreciate his motive for it all, and his love for me. *"Therefore a man shall leave his father and his mother, and shall cleave unto his wife and they shall be one flesh." Genesis 2:24 KJV*

Not one of my family members was in my wedding. I asked months before the wedding three of my sisters to be my maids of honor and brides maids. Neither one of them said yes. My father was very sick at the time and was unable to travel to walk me down the aisle. I also asked my sister and brother from Mississippi to come and sing and bring my baby sister who had no car at the time.

No Longer Bound

They agreed. I asked my best friend to be my matron of honor and she agreed, also from Mississippi. I was so happy until the day of the wedding. I left the house early for my hair appointment and I guess that's when the calls flooded in. My future husband and all his military friends were at my house getting dressed when Brett got the call that none of my family from Mississippi were coming. It still hurts just talking about it now! I remember a few minutes before the wedding started I kept sending people out to check, "Did my family and friends make it yet?" They all knew they weren't coming. So again ten minutes later I sent them out again. "Shirley," I asked, "Did my family make it yet?" So gently she told me, "Airyka, everyone's waiting. We have to start the wedding." I refused to start while waiting on my family. Finally my girls in my wedding sweetly broke it to me that no one could make it. Wow....the disappointment on my big day, but I had a church full of friends, co-workers and even my girlfriend Sarah from Wisconsin had flown back for my wedding. So in a bitter sweet fashion I proceeded. I must say my husband's mother and her husband came in from Carolina. We were both thrilled.

At 3 P.M., I went out to walk down the aisle with a very good friend of mine Larry. I cried and tried to smile on my big day. The moment, Larry gave my hand to Brett, I was fine. He began to hold me and we walked as one of my favorite songs played "You Light Up My Life" sung by Tami Anderson, who has an awesome voice. I remember a serenity coming over me as she sang and finally I transcended to "my moment, our moment" in time. I later learned that night as Brett and I got dressed for our second reception he told me how he'd confided in the wedding party to keep me happy and not allow me to find out before the wedding

51

about my family. I thought, wow, the lengths he went to, to keep me happy that day. It must have been so hard for him. He was as disappointed as I was, however two of my sister's who lived right there in town did show up, thank heavens!

I was so happy. Together we have five children. He had three girls, ages three, five and seven. I had a girl three and a boy five and a dog named Fluffy! Goodness, how do I explain how happy I was to have my own guy, my own husband who loved me and my children? For once I was the center of someone's attention and someone's life. I was a wife!

We had many weekends at Madison Lake and at the park. The kids loved one another. We had huge birthday parties for each of them. Our first Christmas together was so Zenith! Brett bought me a baby doll that Christmas and I got to comb her hair! Yes, we were at a high point in life! I remember one Saturday afternoon looking out of my bedroom window seeing my husband and all five kids out back on a tree swing Brett had made for them. I stood at the window and cried tears of joy! I had a family of my own! I was so appreciative for what Brett had brought to our lives.

Finally the summer of '95 hit. We were having barbeque at the house almost every weekend and going to the lake again with all the kids. When the children were either at their friends' house, or visiting elsewhere, we would take advantage of that time and go out dancing. We tried to enjoy our free time together. On the way out one evening, he commented, "Oh, we have to stop by the bank for money." I answered, "Oh, its ok I have money." First red flag, I can't remember his exact words as he hit the brakes, "Where did you get money?" I looked over at him and stated, "I work." Oh, boy! We had a heated discussion before going out dancing. Believe it or not, I always asked God to protect me and keep me, even in the club or bar scene. Remember God didn't leave me, "I" chose to step away from Him. I knew I was going to be there one day and God also knew I would eventually be out of there one day "*Lo I am with you always, even until the end of the world Amen." Matthew 28:20 KJV*

As time went on we continued with our "happy lives". Shortly before Christmas, my husband received orders to report to Germany by May 1996. We were all happy about the news to have an opportunity to experience a different country! Weeks later, we got passports for ourselves and my two children. My stepdaughters were still under the care of their mother who by now had remarried also. We took time before leaving, going off to our new lives to go and visit as much of the family and friends as we possibly could, not knowing when we would see them again. I really thought I was happy and ready to leave everything else behind until the night before we were headed to the airport. I began to cry telling Brett I felt as though I had lost everything I worked so hard for. I felt as though I'd lost my "blankets", my security, and "my turf". Now I'm in this for real and for good! I was frightened to have to depend on someone once again, especially a man, any man!

Chapter Eight

Germany

Surviving The Storm

It was the first of May when we arrived in Frankfort, Germany. My children and I were in a place I really never dreamed of! It took us hours after arrival to get processed into the country. Shortly after noon we were bused to our duty station, "Stuggart, Germany." We arrived there around 4 P.M. We were taken to the in processing unit for an hour or so to receive instructions for the next day to process with the military. They also assigned us a hotel for two weeks until we found housing. Just to give you a little background, you are shown different areas to accommodate your needs. Say if you needed two bedrooms there are specific housing areas for you. We needed three bedrooms and were authorized to live off base for larger housing, because the Americans said no housing was available. Well, having a German last name sure came in handy, because the German lady working at the housing office heard them tell my husband no housing was available. She came over and said, "Herr Edwards (which is Mr. Edwards in American) I have housing for you." It was forty five kilometers, which is approximately thirty miles from base. It was huge! Three

54

bedroom apartment, with washer and dryer in basement, along with a special cage you were assigned for storage. We were on the fourth floor.

Our children went to an American school in town. They made friends, of course, very fast. Addison swiftly picked up the local language within a month. That came in handy, because my husband left two weeks after getting us into housing. I also had to pass the German written driver's exam which was very hard! But I didn't have a choice! I either passed it or didn't drive. There were no grace periods, it was do or die! So I "did".

While my husband was off training for six weeks at Hohenfels, Germany I was trying to get adjusted to my new life, like the roads and the speed limit that didn't exist on the autobahn. I did not like driving so fast, and very small towns had thirty five to forty kilometers through the neighborhood for safety.

My husband returned after six weeks. I had learned how to get back to base and check the mail. We had post office boxes assigned and I now knew where the commissary and PX were. My husband then informed me he was on orders for Bosnia for approximately a year! I was devastated, hurt, mad, and sad all at once. Brett was awesome about trying to keep us informed of possibilities to deploy so I wasn't caught by total surprise, but hoped it wouldn't come to pass. A week later the military wives were at the gym, waving our little American flags saying goodbyes to our husbands. I was bawling my eyes out. The kids had said their goodbyes the night before and that morning before school. A month or so after he left, I started looking for a job, and I got one. I got a job with the Post Exchange "PX" I wanted to stay

Airyka Edwards

busy and preoccupied. The kids adjusted well with new friends, our son played soccer and Addison in Cheer (gymnastic classes). Thursdays was pizza night for the three of us. We basically stayed to ourselves. Time flew by and Brett was coming back home. I went to one FRG support meeting simply to see when exactly my husband would return. The drama at those meetings was horrific!

Brett returned home, after the first deployment. The kids and I were so happy to have him back in one piece, but he seemed somewhat distant. I began to think maybe he met someone and no longer wanted our family any more or maybe he saw a lot over there and just didn't know how to handle it mentally, which he stated was the issue. I remember us just talking one day in the kitchen and he seemed almost angry then and he asked if I was ok. I said, "Yes just trying to give you some space since you've come home." I remember him asking if I and the kids liked it there and the truth just flew out of my mouth! I said "No, not really. I hate it here!" Oh boy anger turned into more anger! He asked why I hadn't saved any money with the extra money from deployments. I told the truth once again and I felt I was punished for that. I told him "You said, knock out as many bills as you can and don't spend all the money." So I put extra money on every credit card we had. We had accumulated quite a bit of debt since getting married, buying a new car, new furniture, paying for the wedding on another card. So I would place an extra two hundred dollars or more on each. Well, he meant pay bills, save money and pay off cards. Remember I'm not good at math, but I bought nothing new for a year. On top of paying child support for his three girls, sending extra money for their cheer, band and dental work, I did the best I knew to do.

56

No Longer Bound

Christmas came around and my step daughters all wanted a TV with VCR attached and wide legged pants along with other requests. I managed to buy it all for about six hundred dollars or so, plus one hundred dollars to mail it all back to the states. I tried never to neglect his girls in anyway because they didn't deserve that. After Christmas, Brett got orders again to go to Kosovo and Kuwait; I was saddened again, to see him leave. Things had just started to balance and we had to adjust to being alone again, another long year of deployment.

By now, I had switched jobs on base to Save a Center Rent a Car. I met so many new soldiers coming in. After in processing, renting a car was often their next stop, especially if they had families. When the soldier was out processing, going back to the states, I was their last stop, two weeks before leaving. Their vehicle and household goods are shipped months before leaving the country. The soldiers all befriended me to ensure they would get a car on Fridays. Fridays meant going to Amsterdam, Paris, Rome and other countries that were just hours away. Some of the soldiers who worked at the mess hall would even bring or send me lunch, a huge plate of food. One week, several guys bought me tickets for a cruise on the Rhine River! I didn't want to offend any of them so I accepted the tickets. I must have had five or six tickets given to me valued at one hundred dollars each. Many of them said, "Mrs. Edwards, you need to get out and enjoy yourself. So please go, we'll take care of you and won't let anyone harm or hurt you." Truly, those guys would have done anything for me, because I also took care of them.

The weekend came for the cruise and I did not show to board on the boat. The next week I just told the guys I didn't want to leave

57

my children for the weekend. They understood. About a month later while visiting with my husband on the phone he asked if I went on the cruise, I stated, "No." He replied, "Good! Sweetheart, half of our Platoon's wives were on that boat and hugged up with other soldiers, sitting on their laps, kissing, drinking and etc." Brett said, "Dear, I'm so glad you didn't go." I'm thinking I am too, but how does he know all this? Someone videotaped the entire weekend! In the following months many separations, divorces, breakups and even pregnancies came to pass! It was a "Who's your daddy?" weekend. I must admit I use to look down on women that did things like that, but I soon found out why they did what they did. Loneliness was the root of all evil in Germany. I do not condone cheating, but I understand why. I've always said if you leave that country with a "wife" or "rank" you have had a successful tour! Some soldiers came back to empty houses, no car, no money and their families packed up and gone. They could not endure the long span of deployments. The emptiness you feel is horrific! Those who did endure and welcomed their husband's home sometimes wished they hadn't come back. The guys were used to living one way and the families had adjusted to another way of life; "coping while in survival mode" with the mind to serve our husbands and defend ourselves. Often times the guys and some gals were so tired of being deployed, anger was constantly, and always lingering.

My husband came back, finally two months early and he wanted to know how it happened. Well, his mother and her husband were coming overseas to visit for a month and I wasn't entertaining them alone. His commander was processing back stateside and needed a vehicle. I told him when he put my husband on orders for early return and I got a call to confirm he could have a car! The deal worked! Once again happy for his return, with my in-laws visiting, we were fighting again, but I was supposed to keep a smiling, and I did. I had gotten really good at faking Brett always made a point to hurt me and make me cry before a big event. I can recall every trip we'd taken, Paris, Luxemburg, Spain, Mexico, cruises, concerts, you name it, and Brett would find a reason to have me in tears. I can be a "blonde" at times; and I never understood why, it took me a while to catch on. As time traveled I decided it was a control issue he possessed, keep in mind I was not an angel, at least not all of the time. I will be the first to say there were many times I didn't like my husband, but remember there were also times I gave him reasons not to like me. There were many times I did things as a wife that I shouldn't have. I recall being so angry with my husband one day in our bedroom I was trying to discuss something with him, he said his piece and "tried" to walk off. My anger got the best of me; I grabbed a lamp and whipped it so hard across his head and back. I think he saw "stars and Jesus" that day! Am I proud of that? My goodness no! I should have never raised a hand to my husband! Trust me when I say he is a strong retired military man. My husband could have easily taken me out, not only would I have seen stars, but I would have met Jesus if he had even touched me!

There were moments my loneliness got the best of me. I recall once being at work sitting at my desk and a civilian worker came in. He frequently came to visit; he'd talk about his family and I'd speak of mine. He would visit at least once or twice during the week on slow days at the car rental place. One day I recall he walked in, came behind the desk and whispered in my ear, "I

Airyka Edwards

want to be with you Airyka Edwards." I took a deep breath and said, "No, please don't." In reality, I wanted that boy to just kiss me and hold me. Now don't sit there and say oh my goodness I thought she was better than that! I was human just like you and I was lonely just like anyone else. He actually kissed me on the neck after whispering to me and I stood up rapidly and said, "You have to go!" When I went home that night I felt like I had committed the ultimate sin. Although I didn't allow it to go any further my point is I wanted to. You may say, "But Airyka, you stopped it before it went too far." But let me tell you the deed was done way before it happened. Sin is sin. I thought of how bad I wanted him, a touch, a kiss or more. "*So as a man thinketh in his heart so is he.*" Proverbs 23:7 KJV I should have cut him off in his tracks, but I didn't.

There were also times my husband accused me of adultery when I know I was innocent. Brett asked a mutual friend of ours over there to look after his family while he was gone. Just so happened every time Brett called, Santos was there. Bless Santos's heart. Santos was an American who chose to stay and reside in Germany after his military career. He had a couple of demons, alcohol and women, particularly German women. As God is my witness I wouldn't have been with Santos if he was the last guy on earth. I would have just said, "Now Lord, I choose to be alone." (Laugh)

As time went on, I craved my husband. I craved companionship and attention. By now it was November 1998 and I got a call one night about three in the morning. My children's grandmother called to tell me their biological father was very ill. She asked if I would please call him and let the children talk to him. I had so many mixed emotions about that. She also told me he needed

60

their social security numbers. I readily told her no! A few years prior, Tony had gotten our son's social and filed taxes. He had not paid any child support or helped me in any way. I managed by working a second job at Wal-Mart while working at the nursing home. So however, a day or two had gone by and I asked my husband if he was ok with me allowing the children to call. He stated he had no problem with that. I called and put my son on the phone. They talked about ten minutes. Later it was Addison's turn. I told her who it was on the phone. She said, "Hello, this is Addison." Tony said, "Hi, Addison, this is your dad." She said, "My dad! That's not true. I don't know who you are, but my dad is here in Germany!" and she hung up on him! "Ouch". I called him back and apologized for her. "After all she was only a few weeks old when we separated." She really didn't know him.

A week went by and I received another phone call Tony had passed away from heart disease. I also got another call a day later from Red Cross "your father is ill and need you to come home." My mind is racing, what do I do? My husband had previously told me, "I have raised those children and they are my children and I'm their father now." I had no beef with that except in that same breath, he stated if something happened and he died the children weren't going to his funeral. I thought number one Tony said he was dying and that he didn't have long to live. I honestly didn't believe him. Our history wasn't great or should I say his history with telling me the truth wasn't great. So I thought he's lying. No one's dying. He even went on to say, "I left everything to my children." My thoughts were "Yeah right." Well Brett was adamant about me or the kids going stateside. I made a decision to get a return flight stateside on orders from my father being sick. My husband told

Airyka Edwards

me he would not get me orders to go stateside for any reason. Well don't ever tell a woman that, when she has determination! At that point I didn't think my husband knew me that well. I left our apartment, went to the processing center, walked in, spoke with a civilian I'd helped numerous times and simply said, "I need orders please for three round trip tickets stateside to land in Mississippi." I had tickets in my hand in less than fifteen minutes. Remember it pays to be kind even on days you don't have it in you. It's who you know, not what!

The kids and I drove to Mississippi and spent the day with my dad. My dad said, "Baby, I heard the children's father died and sweetheart you need to go." I told my dad I had come home on orders to take care of him. He said, "Sweetheart, I'm going to be fine. Now go to Louisiana and close that chapter in your life." My dad was such an amazing dad. He sat himself aside for me. My dad remembered every Thanksgiving Tony and I would come visit him and Christmas, We'd go visit Tony's mother and family also.

The next day, Friday, the children and I had a rental car and drove to Southern, Louisiana; one of the most unpleasant smelling towns in the state due to the local paper mill. We arrived and visited with Tony's mother and other family members. The next morning, Saturday, we buried the children's biological father. That was so avenging for me! I was kind of numb. I was hurt, mad, and even sad he died, but really didn't connect his passing with eternity never seeing him in this life again. It was surreal! I know I was in shock and I hated to see his lifeless body lying there in that of piece of equipment, and yet it was his body's final resting place.

62

No Longer Bound

We managed to make it through the day. Tony had been adopted by his biological father and his wife. We had the "not so good" pleasure of meeting Tony's biological mother. My children were somewhat confused. She seemed so happy to meet Tony's children however this lady hadn't seen her own son alive and well, since he was around six or seven years old, the same age as my son was at this time. I remember how bad Tony at times wanted to see her or just talk to her, but she would never return a letter or call from him. That was the source of a lot of hurt in him. My mind was racing as this lady began to lie to my children; I grabbed them both and said, "Let's get to the car. It's waiting on us." She vowed to keep in touch with them. It's history; thank heavens, they have never heard from her. I never allowed people to get that close to my children to lie or hurt them. A day later we headed back to my dad's house, over two and a half hours away. He was so happy to see us. We cleaned my dad's house then went and bought groceries for him. When we left, we all reeked of lemon pine sol.

We visited with some of my family for a few days. My brother from Chicago was there trying to sort his life out after his divorce from twenty plus years of marriage. It finally came time to leave and go back to Germany. I had to face the reality now of my decision. As we arrived at Frankfort, my husband was there to receive us and quickly asked, "Well, did you go to the funeral?" I had to say, "Well, Brett if I say we went, you'll be mad and if I say we didn't you'll think you won." So my final answer was, "Let's not ever bring this up again."

We tried moving on, days and weeks went by as more problems arose. I'd lost my libido, which I believe a lot of women or men experience some time or another in life. It is when a woman loses her desire to be intimate with her spouse. Sometimes certain medications can cause this; blood pressure medications, oral contraceptives, antihistamines, menopause hormone changes, and antidepressants. Stress is a huge factor. It is sometimes just part of life changes with our bodies as we age. It may be embarrassing to speak of or talk about with your spouse or friend, but there are certainly worse things in life! I finally confessed to my husband that I was filing for a divorce. I was not taking anything from him or expecting anything of him, but I no longer wanted him to touch me. I told him my heart loved him so dearly and he deserved better. I'd said all this in a three page letter and told him by the next week I was going back stateside. We literally did not speak or talk for days and the day I started to pack little did I know Brett was in the living room, crying. He is about to lose yet another family. He approached the bedroom with reddish eyes and red face, gave me the biggest hug and said, "Please don't leave. I love you and I don't care if we're never intimate again. You and the kids are my life." That really didn't move me much, because I thought well, this will wear off in a few weeks. I gave him the opportunity to accept my offer again, "Let me go. I take nothing or I'll stay and you never throw this situation in my face nor bring it back up if you are willing to accept me as is." He held on tighter. He knew my strength. At this point I was strong "from within". Again he asked, "Dear, please don't leave me. I love you and the kids. I'll accept you. You are the best wife and the best thing that ever happened to me." Wow, where I got that true courage, I don't know, but it got stronger through the years as I faced more disappointments and tragedies in my life. I began to "gain, retain, and absorb" more inner strength.

No Longer Bound

It was time to pack for our stateside return! Only God Himself knew how happy I was about that! We received orders for Louisiana. Where it would take others weeks and sometimes months to pack for PCS move, it only took me days! My husband knew once again he would have to leave just weeks after arrival. And so it was, we returned to the great USA!! The day after arrival we were at the in processing waiting room, watching television. They kept showing Colorado. We didn't know what happened or what was going on. In Germany we had one American channel and the events were at least one month behind. Confusion set in, so we asked if what we were seeing was "now". A person responded, "Yes." Someone shot and killed several students at Columbine High school. Oh my, I thought, umm Germany looks better already I hated our tour there, because my husband was gone most of the time. I must say Germany is one of the most beautiful countries on earth!

The best part of our tour while in Germany was meeting my husband's European family. His Uncle Wolfgang was the mayor of the town they resided in, in Germany. His great aunt we met, was around ninety two years old although she had lost most of her eyesight, it seemed as if she could see us all. She smiled and smiled. She was one of the most pleasant women I'd ever met. Brett's other aunt, Uncle Wolfgang's wife was, Sara Ann, a sweet, beautiful and a classy lady. Cousin Patti and her brother were all very nice and attentive. They stated they wanted to take us out to eat that evening to meet a few more family members. And my husband said he had a small family! When we arrived at the restaurant it was table after table all connected around the restaurant reserved especially for the Edwards and Wolfgang family, it was about fifty more people! They all stood and clapped

Airyka Edwards

welcoming us. They took hundreds of photos and fed us well. They were mesmerized over how pretty Addison was. They thought the kids looked like pure chocolate candy. We had the best time ever! I remember leaving their house after two to three days of being well taken care of. I tried to be nice and left a card with three hundred dollars in German marks. My husband told me not to do that, that they'd be highly offended. Well in America people love that. Needless to say they met us at the Frankfort Airport the day of our stateside departure and handed me the money back. They said in broken English/German, "When you "wisit us", we take care of you. When we "wisit you", you take care of us. That's the way it works!" I looked at them and said ok and "Das tut mir leid", which is to say, I'm sorry. We all smiled and gave lots of hugs before we departed. I paid Cousin Patti a compliment and said I love your blouse! Well, she took it off right there in the middle of the airport and gave it to me! Luckily she had a jacket with her! Laugh! Yes, be careful what you say! .....And so we departed.

Chapter Nine

Louisiana – Part I

The Worst Pain I'd Ever Felt --- Losing My Dad

Once again we charted off to a new beginning in Louisiana. After arriving back in the states, we started visiting family; my family and then his girls for a few days in Texas. We drove to see my dad and my mom. I told them I'd be back in a few weeks to get my dad's place together. My brother had helped my dad move into a house. My husband had previously asked for a compassionate assignment so I could be only hours away to go back and forth to care for my dad who was now eighty four.

We drove to Louisiana to pick up our new vehicle that we had ordered before leaving Europe. A few days after receiving housing we had to get the kids back in school for the last few weeks to complete their school year. They finished school that year in Slidell, Louisiana with their grandmother, Tony's mother. Brett and I returned to the Military base to receive household goods and set up house. He had orders for school in two weeks in Alabama. We rushed around and got everything set up and then he left. It took me a few days to realize I didn't have a vehicle

67

Airyka Edwards

until I went out to the driveway to hop in the truck. So I rented a car for a few days. I called my husband to ask if he'd look for a convertible, for my "midlife crisis." He found me one in about a week; of course I had to fly to Alabama so I could drive it back. I hate to fly just like I hate snakes but I had to so off I went. While visiting my husband in Alabama we drove to visit his mother for a day or two which wasn't too far off. She piled our Durango with household stuff; bedspreads, televisions, kitchen items and more! I love mother-in-laws. All that had to fit in my car to return to Louisiana.

It was Monday evening and Brett was still at the Chemical School House for training. He would be back to the room about 5:15 P.M. and then around 4:00 it hit me like a freight train! I began to cry so hard my eyes were swollen. I tried to control myself but grief took over as if something bad had just happened. We'd called my father the day before, after returning from North Carolina visiting Brett's mom. My dad seemed fine. I hurriedly dried my face before Brett got home that evening, but as soon as he walked through the door he looked at me and said, "Dear, what's wrong?" Very slowly he asked, "Did I say something? Did I do something?" I shook my head fast, saying, "No, no, no it's not you! We're fine." I said, "It's my dad!" He stated, "Sweetheart, we just spoke with him yesterday. He's fine." I said, "I know, but I've had a "premonition" and it's not good!" He held me close and said, "Sweetheart, let's hope this is wrong." I said, "Ok" and dismissed the whole idea.

"Premonition"- Abnormal or Anxious feeling over a future event. A feeling of danger, fearful expectation and sometimes anticipation or even Feelings or belief that something bad or unforeseen is going to happen when there is no definite knowledge.

No Longer Bound

Yes, the Lord could have been talking to me, but at that time in my life, I wasn't in line with the Lord to even hear his voice. So take it as you may.

We went to eat that night with new friends of Brett's whom he'd met while in school in Alabama. They became very close family friends, Miguel and Pat Speig. We had a fabulous time getting to know each other and reminiscing about our Germany tour. Miguel's wife, Pat is German. We were all on the same tour, but never connected. The night ended and I was to leave for Louisiana early Tuesday morning around 4 A.M. to get a jump start on traffic. I'd planned to stop in Mississippi on my way to spend a few hours with my dad.

I left Alabama and arrived in Mississippi approximately at 7:30 A.M., stopping at Charlie's Chicken and got four thighs and two jalapeño peppers for my dad. He loved chicken like any Southerner. It was only about a minute to his house from Charlie's. I pulled up ready to show my dad my new white Chrysler Lebaron and was ready to take him for a ride in it after I unloaded some stuff. My daddy wasn't on the front porch as he always had been anywhere he lived. He was always up by 6 A.M. and made his breakfast, and still made his coffee in a percolator. I bought him a new one, but he never used it. He always finished his coffee on the porch, watching people. By now I'm in shock, he is not outside! I immediately called my husband on his cell and told him, "My dad's not outside honey! He's not out here!" Brett says, "Dear, calm down, maybe he's taking a bath." "No!" I said, "He takes his bath at night!" He said, "Maybe your sister or brother took him somewhere. So just go knock." I told Brett I'd call him back. I went to knock on the door, but no answer. I banged on the door, but

69

Airyka Edwards

still, no answer! I went to his bedroom window to the left of the porch. I can barely see, but I saw him in bed! I yelled "Dad please, just open the door and I'll take care of you!" He was lying on his back rocking up and down trying to get up! He called out once, "I can't baby. Help me!" I'd never broken into anything, especially not anyone's house, so I thought what do I do? I ran to my car and grabbed my purse, took a credit card out, I'd seen this done on TV. I got the door open with it! I went to my dad's room and he said, "I'm sick baby, real sick." I panicked! I said, "No, no, you just need some water and your medicine." I brought that to him and went to make him some coffee. I started a tub of water. He had had an accident and soiled his pajamas and bedding. He said, "Baby, you gotta call for help!" I remember saying, "Why? Dad, if you just drink your coffee you will feel better!" Fear set in so bad! By now I knew if I acknowledged he was sick, this might be it! The bath water was still running and I had brought the chicken in, with my purse and placed on the television. I rapidly closed the door to his bedroom, picked up his house phone and dialed 911. "911 may I help you?"…silence…. "Hello, may I help you?" Yes my dad!" My mouth closed and I stopped breathing. They picked up the address by an added service on the phone I had for my dad. I never said another word…..I recall the ambulance pulling up, lights flashing and sirens going. I believe my heart stopped that day! I was totally deprived of any sensation. I feel like I had been given an anesthetic, feeling so immobile. The paramedics asked me questions but I couldn't talk. I tried, honest to God, I tried! The water was still running in the tub. Finally the paramedics started an IV drip and gave him meds and asked me about allergies. I was speechless, until they were about to place him on the stretcher and I remember yelling, "Don't you dare! You give him dignity

No Longer Bound

clean him up!" I found underwear and clean pajamas. I'd done his laundry about two weeks earlier. They obliged me and cleaned him up. By now the tub had run over and one of the paramedics turned the water off. We left the house. I called Brett and again all I remember is saying, "My dad" and I hung up! We arrived around 8 A.M. at the Memorial Hospital. They worked on my dad for about one and a half hours before letting me in the room. I had just enough time to catch my breath. I know he's okay and they are going to take good care of him, I kept thinking because if not, this "new strength" I began to obtain in Germany will kick in!

The doctors and nurses talked to me and said he was in CHF-in medical terms, "Congestive Heart Failure" and had a massive amount of fluid in him. They spent hours aspirating fluid from his lungs. They even broke needles on him. He was a diabetic and sometimes diabetic's skin can be like leather, it's so tough. After a couple of hours had gone by, I was still sitting right by his bedside. After dosing off and on he woke up and said, "Baby, is that you?" I said, "Yes, Dad it's me." He said, "I knew you'd save me. Baby, if you hadn't stopped by I would have died!" I smiled and said, "Dad, that's the one thing you better not do to me, is leave me. I love you and I still need you in my life." He laughed, "Baby, I ain't going anywhere until the good Lord's ready for me!" so I teasingly said, "Well, I hope He has gone on to somebody else's room!" The curtain was cracked a little in my dad's room and one of the local cops peaked over and saw my dad and came in to speak. "Hey Buster, how you doing old timer?" My dad laughed, "Hey Big "O". Make your acquaintances with my daughter. The cop turned and looked at me, he said, "Buster, you ain't got no daughter that looks this good!" It just warmed my dad's heart

71

Airyka Edwards

someone flirting with his child. "Back off" he said, "she's taken already!" He laughed again, Good to see you Ole Timer, and the cop exited the room. My dad looks over and winks, "Baby, that ole boy wanted my baby." He laughed. I said, "Dad, nobody's trying to flirt with your daughter", but I smiled. Hours later about 4 P.M. my dad said, "Baby, it's about time for you to get on that road now to Louisiana. I said, "Dad, I'm not leaving until you leave!' He said," Baby, I'm fine." I repeated, "No I'm fine too. I'm not leaving." I told him to just lay there and rest. At approximately 9 P.M. He was moved to a room in "CCU" not "ICU"- critical care unit, the unit for the worst of the worst. They took about another hour to stabilize him and allowed me fifteen more minutes. I was assured he was fine and I was totally exhausted! It was approaching 10:30 P.M. so I called my mom to ask if I could stay over explaining that my dad was very ill. She said come on over. I showered and laid on her couch in fresh clothes in case I had to leave in a hurry. (I'd learned that from my mom years before.)

I remember falling asleep fast, as I was mentally and physically drained! It was 3:02 A.M. when my mother's phone rang. I jumped up and grabbed the phone; once again I went into shock. The nurse said, "Airyka Edwards, your dad has taken a turn for the worse. Get here ASAP!" I hung up as the lady was still talking. My mother got out of her bed and came into the living room to check on me. I managed to tell her, "My dad I, gotta go." She grabbed me and hugged me! I believe it was the first time "I was age thirty five" at that time that she said, "Honey, do you need me? I will come with you." I said, "No, I'll be fine. He always comes out right. This time just seemed a little rougher than other times."

No Longer Bound

I made it to the hospital where the doctor stopped me in the hall to say "Your father coded, but we used measures, he'd asked for in his living will. I was in a panic by now and they set me down and talked to me before they let me in to see him. I listened, but never heard a word! Finally, they let me in his room. I ran over to kiss him and held his hand in mine. I put his cold hand on my face and kissed his hands. I talked to him and hoped he heard me. I continued to just set on his bed, and then laid my head on his chest that was only rising because of being on a ventilator (life support) that was breathing for him. His eyes were half mast. I rubbed his face telling him, "Dad I'm sorry I left. I was just so tired, but I'm here now and I promise I won't leave again. Daddy, please wake up to just tell me you're okay, please."

It was June 15th, the doctor kept telling me I needed to make a decision about "when" not "if" I was going to allow them to pull the plug and let him go! I looked straight into the doctor's eyes and said, "I will not, nor can I tell you to take him off! He will wake up just give him a few more hours! By now my sister had come to the hospital. My mother called to tell her what was going on. Next my best friend, Marion came. It was approaching 2:45 and Marion had to go to work in a few minutes. Later my sister got cold and went out to her patrol car to get her jacket; she's a police officer. At 3 P.M. the doctor came in to say, "We are taking him off. We gave him his last wish." Seconds later the doctor turned the machine off! I was crying and screaming, "No, please! No just wait till my sister comes back up." He said, "No, ma'am we have to go forward with this." He pulled the plug out of the wall and my dad's chest stopped rising! I remember vaguely laying across my dad holding him and crying, "Daddy, I'm sorry! I'm sorry! I failed you!"

Airyka Edwards

My sister returned asking, "What happened, what happened sis?" I said, "He's heartless. He took my dad, Sis He took my dad!" Oh goodness, I was devastated once again in my life, but now I was really lost. I had no father and no one to take care of! I'd moved this close for him! The rest of the day the funeral home people called me to ask if I would come down to make arrangements. I said, "No! I won't come down." He said, "Ma'am can I come to you, please?" I agreed. That Wednesday I planned the home going for my dad. I was so lost my heart had emptiness like never before. My head was spinning and I remember I hadn't called my husband or my children who were still in Louisiana with their grandmother. I made those painful calls. I remember my poor son saying, "Mommy I'm sorry you lost your dad. I know how you feel though being that I lost my real dad a few months ago." I began bawling my eyes out! My child is consoling me! Marion, my friend, drove me back to the base in Louisiana to get clothes for my family. I wasn't stable enough to drive. I left my car parked at my mother's house. I truly don't remember how it got there.

We set the funeral service for the following Saturday. Brett drove to Mississippi from Alabama. The children and their grandmother came from Louisiana. My sister, Martha and brother-in-law came from Texas. I had showed up at the funeral home on Friday to view and approve my dad's departure. I hate funeral homes. They creep me out! I was there by 3 P.M. The viewing would begin for the public at 5 P.M. Along with my oldest sister, and my mother, we went to the Funeral home. We were escorted to the chapel where Dad's body lay and my sister told me the next day I walked in and dropped! She said I fainted as I took my sunglasses off. Gosh, this is one difficult chapter I must face this lonely road God

No Longer Bound

has sent me down. I manage to make it through the morning getting dressed. I was at the hotel with my husband, who had made it in on Friday night.

We got to my mother's house where the limo was picking my family up. Lo and behold, there were a few people at my mom's house waiting to follow the family car. One person in particular was Odessa! Yes, the girl that whipped my tail in the seventh grade. I remember looking at my sister asking out loud, "What is she doing here?" My sister took me outside and said, "Duke, that's what my sister called me, Odessa knew your dad and she's had a stroke. Just leave her alone." I said, "Perfect time for me to whip her for a little payback!" I wasn't smiling then, but now I am! I calmed down and we went to church. The funeral director looked at me and asked who I had named for pallbearers. I said, "I don't know." I didn't know I had to take care of that, it triggered another round of tears. He said, "Ma'am, it's okay, we'll take care of it. So they gathered my husband, my brother, and two guys from the funeral home. My dad's service was very nice. The preacher was good from what I remember. At the closing of the service, they opened Dad's casket for a final viewing. I got up to pay my very last respects to my best man, the man that loved me more than anything and cherished his only child. I went up. I barely made it with people on each side holding me. I was so weak; I hadn't eaten for a week. They had closed the casket on me due to them thinking I could not handle it. So I did not get my time I needed to say goodbye. My heart still bleeds today. I crave just to see my dad, just to hug him and his big belly I so loved. He once told me he was so proud of me for learning to drive and getting my license. He always said I belonged working in a hospital

Airyka Edwards

taking care of people like the nurses took care of him through the years. I have a photo of him and my stepmother in the drawer of my night stand for the last fifteen years and have not been able to look nor place it on my stand next to my bed. The strongest man I knew was gone. Never in thirty five years have I hung up the phone or walked out of a room without saying, "I love you, Daddy!" His response was always, "I love you, too, baby!"

The next day was Sunday, Fathers Day, We (my family and some friends) had gone to Wal-Mart for some reason, but when we all arrived everyone said their goodbyes to me. My kids, their grandmother and aunt, my niece, my sister and brother-in-law, lastly my husband, I asked why everyone had to leave me right then. In reality they knew it wasn't going to be a good day for me. And yes, I hate Father's Day!

By Monday I started to think, my goodness, I have to clear my dad's house out and get utilities disconnected. I was starting to get overwhelmed again! I asked my sister and brother to please come help me. They came over and I remember walking in and seeing the chicken on the TV and I broke down again. I pulled myself together and proceeded to pack items, finishing up in a couple days. We lived on base so I didn't have room to take anything with me. However, I did ask my brother to hold on to my dad's wardrobe for a few months and I would find a place for it. My brother and his girlfriend moved several times in six months never telling me, so they left Dad's things and lost the one thing he'd actually cherished that I wanted so badly. I have small things, a few ceramic pieces and cookie jars.

No Longer Bound

In November 1999, my family and I were invited to have Thanksgiving with my Aunt Anna and Uncle Claude in Alabama. We drove there from the base in Louisiana. My children were especially happy, because they loved to visit family. While driving I asked my husband to pull off on Lyle Street to see my stepmother. No answer, but I left a note on the door telling her we'd stop on the way back in a few days. We had a wonderful time in Alabama with family. On our return trip back home we stopped once again at my stepmother's. The note was gone. I called, but no answer. I left another note, and so we drove back to Louisiana.

My stepmother had come to my dad's funeral and I was very happy to see her. My husband wanted to see where I had grown up that part of my life, so the day after my dad's funeral we went to visit her. We all sat outside and my kids asked her questions about me when I was younger. She looked at my husband and said, "I helped raise her you know that, right?" My husband said, "Yes ma'am, she speaks of you a lot." She told him I was a good child. Minutes later she looked over at me and said, "Duke, I want to apologize. I know I wasn't the best mother and I know Jacob used to torture you. I wish you'd told me all those years." I said, "Its ok." She said, "No baby, it's not. I'm sorry." I asked her how she'd ever found out. She replied, "Jacob told me after you left and he felt bad and he truly missed you." (Understand this is twenty-three years later, but she had the courage to say all this to me.) I told her, "You have no idea how good that makes me feel and thank you so much for discussing this with me.

I had been going to her house with my dad and the children's father, "Tony" during Thanksgiving every year, but she never said anything then. Of course my dad was around too and he was

Airyka Edwards

too busy telling her "she never could cook that well". That still tickles me today, as he ate her mushy Jiffy "cornbread" dressing! I tried calling her several times and sent all my Christmas cards the first week of December. After Christmas one day I came home from work and found her card had come back to me, "Resident Deceased" stamped on it! I lay across the bed and was saddened once again for getting cheated out of saying goodbye. God had allowed us months before to make peace and that is how I got through that.

I apparently never healed from the passing of my father until now I realized I have never asked God for healing. I think I wanted to hurt. I wanted to cry. I never wanted to forget my dad. I had spent years away from Mississippi, for the simple reason I could not bear being in that town without seeing my father. When I do visit I take flowers out and place them on his grave and I'm at peace sitting there talking to him, even though as a Christian I know he is not there. His body is, but my dad is not....or is he? There's a passage in the Bible that says in I *Thessalonians 4: 13-18 KJV: "V 13. But I would not have you to be ignorant, brethren, concerning them which are asleep, that ye sorrow not, even as others which have no hope.*

v. 14. For if we believe that Jesus died and rose again, even so them also which sleep in Jesus wills God bring with him.

v. 15 for this we say unto you by the word of the Lord, that we which are alive and remain unto the coming of the Lord shall not prevent them which are asleep.

No Longer Bound

v. 16 For the Lord himself shall descend from heaven with a shout, with the voice of the archangel, and with the trump of God: and the dead in Christ shall rise first:

v. 17 Then we which are alive and remain shall be caught up together with them in the clouds to meet the Lord in the air: and so shall we ever be with the Lord.

v. 18 Wherefore comfort one another with these words."

So I'm sometimes confused on that. I also have read in my Bible in Ecclesiastes 9:5, "For the living know that they shall die: but the dead know not anything....."

Then we have on the other hand II Corinthians 5:8 KJV "We are confident, I say, and willing rather to be absent from the body, and to be present with the Lord."

Matthew 25:46 KJV "And these shall go away into everlasting punishment: but the righteous into life eternal." (Speaking of the "unjust")

I will probably have this discussion with my pastor.

I know that this chapter was extensive, but I wanted to share when one loses a loved one, healing does not always come right away or in a year or two. I still struggle on letting go and if I let go, once I die, no one will remember my dad or go to his grave or mine.

Airyka Edwards

I truly want to heal and let go. I believe and hope this helps heal someone else. I'm going to ask God now for my healing, for my transformation; "We have not because we ask not."

"And whatsoever ye shall ask in my name, that will I do, that the Father may be glorified in the Son." John 14:13 KJV

Chapter Ten

Our Tour to Louisiana—Part II

Once everyone returned home the first week of July, I'd been alone, still on base for approximately two weeks. I was never so thrilled to see my husband pull up! He stopped on his way back from Texas and picked his three girls up. The next day we went to pick my children up and truthfully, we looked like the Clamppetts on the way back! (Laugh)

Well there was a side of my husband that I loved so dearly. While chatting with my sister Ranne one day on the phone she commenced to tell me about some of our family matters. One other sister, while visiting Mississippi, saw one of my nephews in need of a little TLC, food, shelter, clothes, and so forth, so my sister decided to offer him a better life in Texas with her and her three children. My nephew was ecstatic! He grabbed what few things he owned stuffed them in one bag and was off to Texas. This nephew, Little Terry, belongs to my middle brother Terry. As he began to settle into his new life in Texas, my sister soon began to think, "I can't take care of another child!" She said she was taking him back to Mississippi. As my baby sister and I continued talking I became sad and started to cried. My husband happened

81

to come outside to see what was going on, as he knew it was still fresh for me losing my Dad. I began to try and tell Brett what my other sister had embarked on and now was about to send this kid back to a life she took him out of! He immediately said, "Tell her we're going to get the kid next weekend!" I said, "What?" Brett repeated, "We are going to get the kid next weekend! It's not his fault and it's not fair for her to treat him like that." I have always admired the kind heart Brett has for children and animals. The next weekend we drove to Texas and picked Terry up and it was then he started a new life with us. My son loved having a cousin around like a big brother, as he was the only boy between Brett and I. we took all the kids school shopping even though it wasn't time. Terry was so happy to get new everything! To add to it all we got him a wallet and started him with fifty dollars. However we laid down some rules. He was in the ninth grade and had to work a part time job and get his driver's license. (I had the honor of teaching him to drive.) He had to stay in school, keep an A & B grade average and no smoking or drinking, which Little Terry hated because this is how he ended up with other people, his parents, unable to care for themselves let alone him. He often times would say, "Auntee, my mother don't love me or she would have treated me like you and Uncle Brett." I hurriedly cleared his mind from any negative thoughts. I instantly began to elaborate on how his mother hadn't been loved or cherished by anyone, so I tried to explain to him, "Terry she loves you in the only way she can and the only way she knows how." We taught him no matter how rough things had been you should still, "Honor thy Father and thy Mother that thy days may be long upon the land which the Lord thy God giveth thee" He began to call her as we instructed him to build on what little relationship he had. We encouraged him

No Longer Bound

to call her at least once a month to start. We encouraged him to go see her when we would visit Mississippi and to tell her, "I love you", although the words might be hard to say. Terry had some forgiveness to work on, and hurt over his lack of care growing up and so many other issues, but he worked through those things. Today Terry is about twenty-eight years old, a college graduate with a degree in auto mechanics, has a house and a family of his own. He often tells us, "Auntee, I appreciate you all taking me in because I wouldn't have what I have today if it wasn't for you and my uncle." My brother has also spoken of his appreciation of our love toward his son. I am proud of my nephew today. We love him dearly; another success story of poverty to paradise!

For our "Clamppett" clan, we had a huge barbeque for the Fourth of July and took the kids fishing that day. Sunday we took off and went to a local flea market where they saw this little dog for sale from a lady who didn't know she was a male or female dog. All six of the children knew I wanted a Boston Terra, but instead they kept trying to get me to accept this little mutt they'd found. The kids finally said, "Mommy, just hold her and if you don't want her after that we'll leave you alone, promise!" I said, "Give me the little B-K mutt! The rest is history. I named her Angel. I looked into that dog's eyes and it seemed as though she had my dad's eyes. I knew right away she was going home with us and she would help me through my pain. She's fifteen years old today. I remember fifteen years prior to my dad's passing, (not to get back on the subject, but I need to make a point); I went back to Mississippi to check on him again. He was sick and I was scared. I stopped at my sister's house to tell her I had to leave for Mississippi. I sat on her bed crying and saying "you know if God would just give me fifteen

83

Airyka Edwards

years more……..." Well He did! Be very careful what you ask for, it was fifteen years to the day. I couldn't very well get mad at God, but I tried to be happy with all my family together again.

We had a blast that summer. Our girls got to stay for a month. I remember my oldest step daughter wanting a rabbit, so we got her a rabbit and cage. We went skating, bowling, to the movies and more every weekend. Try doing that with six kids and two adults….and a partridge in a pear tree! We had a great time with our family, but eventually, the summer ended and we drove the girls back to Texas.

While on our journey Louisiana, I visited a few churches, but I saved the best for last. Somehow I knew I'd end up at "IDF"; Interdenomination, Church of the Living God, with Pastor Samuel and Co-Pastor Augustine Ullasys a dynamite duo! They were both "God fed and God led!" I loved the family atmosphere at my church. I was always greeted by my Pastor and First Lady. She has no idea of the impact she made on my life.

I explained earlier how my dad took a turn for the worst receiving a call from the hospital about 3 A.M. and after that for months to follow I couldn't sleep. When I did get to sleep I'd wake up every single morning at 3 A.M. sharp. It was like clockwork. I began to get frustrated. While I was still grieving and couldn't sleep, I lost my stepdad a couple weeks after my dad passed away. I was so stressed! I went to church one Sunday and Co-Pastor Augustine came back to where I stood during altar call and prayer. I just stood at my seat crying, hurting and frustrated, I thought, "God please do something, help me, and deliver me!" Minutes later Co-Pastor Augustine told me no longer will I wake up at 3 A.M;

84

No Longer Bound

God is going to give you peace! I remember just falling to my seat, sobbing and praising God! God heard my prayer because I never told her until afterwards I'd lost my dad and that's why I was waking up at 3 A.M. I told her that was the time associated with my dad's death.

When I love, I love hard. When I fall, I fall hard! My church in Louisiana gave me the strength I needed daily just to function. IDF was my daily manna I needed to survive. Brett and I attended one of the church's annual banquets. It was there that we started to bond and have fun again. Co-Pastor Augustine was up speaking and she said something that triggered our laughing spells. Well, our tickle box turned completely over. Brett and I began to laugh so hard we cried. Finally Co-Pastor Ullasys stated over the microphone, "Bro. and Sis Edwards would you like to share that with the rest of us?" We couldn't talk. We couldn't acknowledge her speaking to us; we were cutting up so bad. Everyone around us began to laugh just as hard, because we couldn't stop! That was the side of my husband I absolutely loved and still do! We finally recovered after about a fifteen minute span, and then she called our names out for winning a Valentine's Day weekend with hotel, dinner and a wonderful couple's book and basket, that we took home.

While in Louisiana, I began job hunting and going to Medical Assistant School. September 11th happened and days later my husband was deployed to the Pentagon in Washington D.C. for two months. He returned and a week later was deployed to Kuwait. Brett wasn't going to be home for Christmas but he was there for Thanksgiving. This Thanksgiving was going to be another hard one for me, being back in the states, but not with my

85

dad. I didn't want my family to suffer. I felt as though I'd put them through enough already. I decided to run the thought by Brett to invite my entire family to visit to keep me preoccupied. It worked, nineteen of my family members came! We had an awesome time. It was such a blessing to have them there supporting me. My husband and I cooked for two days baking and preparing to make sure everyone was accommodated. I remember we made three turkeys: one traditional in oven, one smoked and one deep fried. Normally after Thanksgiving we make turkey soup that would last for about two weeks. That year we didn't have anything left but the carcasses. Days later Brett left again for almost a year. The kids were in school and met new friends. I worked and continued my schooling.

After about a year, I landed a job at a doctor's office. She was an OB-GYN physician. I started working for her before I actually finished my school. Her business was fairly new; as she had only been open approximately three to four months when I was hired. We were only seeing about ten patients a day. The physicians' office where I completed my internship was booming! I started to notice the secretary would only schedule what she felt like for a day. One day Doc and I went out for lunch. I graciously asked, "Why aren't you seeing more patients?" She responded, "I'm not sure, Airyka, but we have to do something to survive." Well my mind immediately went crazy! "You want to talk survival?" I asked, "Doc, do you mind if I intervene some to help?" Her eyes lit up and she said, "Yes what do you have planned?" I asked if she was ready to trust me and work like crazy. She responded, "Yes, Airyka, yes. I said, "Ok, from now on we schedule four people for 8 A.M. two every fifteen minutes. When you walk in the room we will be full to start, clean and fill the rooms as one leaves. Tuesdays were her surgery days so we caught up on paperwork, rescheduling mammograms, calling in scripts, ordering supplies, etc. In about one month we went from ten to thirty to forty patients per day not including deliveries, which she had to run over to the hospital next door to do. On days like those I'd feed everybody in the office that included patients as they waited. She would go to Sam's Club and fill our storage closet at the office with snacks! The patients loved that!

A year and a half had come and gone. We worked like crazy until one day she handed me a huge check! I said, "What is this for?" She replied, "You never took a vacation. You get two weeks a year." I said, "Well, I "forgot" to take a vacation! We were so busy!" That check went fast. I went to see my husband at lunch a couple weeks after he had returned from Iran. I cashed the check and told him to send the money for his daughters (my stepdaughter) braces and the rest for him to get a small fishing boat he wanted and I went back to work as usual. Time moved on. Brett was deployed once again. The kids were getting into their teenage years and started to rebel. They often told me I was really mean when Brett left. After about the third deployment in Louisiana even my nephew said, "Auntie, we hate it when Uncle Brett leaves. With all due respect you get really mean with us for a few weeks every time he leaves." That was hard to swallow, but I took my constructive criticism and built on it. I apologized to the kids and was very conscious of my behavior from then on.

By now the office was booming where I worked and I decided to take on more schooling! What was I thinking? I went to Phlebotomy school I believe it was for six months, two days a

Airyka Edwards

week, 6 to 9 P.M. The last three weeks of school I became very ill with double pneumonia! I was the sickest I had ever been in my adult life. I worked for a physician, so with her permission I nursed myself with every antibiotic I could and did not get any relief, Finally after about two weeks, I missed school one night for the first time while enrolled. I drove myself to the base hospital where they immediately hooked me up with several IV's fluids for my severe dehydration and gave me several breathing treatments and a prescription for more meds that I'd already dowsed into my body! I had to call my nephew to get a ride so he could come get me and our vehicle, as I was too weak to drive. The next day I called into work for the first time in four years of working there. I got the strength to get up and shower. I also made it to my safe to pull out my last will and testament, in case the children would need it; that's how sick I was. The "FRG" leader from the military wives group called to swing by to pick up donations I previously purchased. She was floored by how sick I was and hadn't called for my husband's emergency return. I was mortified when my husband called asking what was going on. I pretended I had no clue of what he was speaking of. Finally I broke the truth and told him I was really ill and didn't know my fate at this time. He asked if I needed him there. I stated, "No! You are working and I will be fine." The kids were helping as much as they could and there was nothing he could do to help me. I asked him if he really knew God, if so, to please pray for my complete healing. I over came that illness by God's own grace.

A few months later my son got in trouble with some boys on base by the "MP" (military police). They were parked in a car after curfew with girls in another car. By now Brett was home. When he punished he punished hard. Our son had four months of no TV, no games, such as play station, no bike, not even a radio. He was left with an alarm clock and bed in his room. I thought that was a little harsh, but at that time he needed harsh because I had a soft spot for him. I've always felt guilty for taking them away from their biological father. He was two years old at the time. Yes, he'd witness his dad's mean side, but remembered that was still his dad. When I moved out on my own, Addison was maybe three months old. She didn't know or remember him. My son would spend nights crying, "Mommy, I am sorry if I made you leave Daddy or if I did something wrong." Boy did that break my heart! So I would set with him and pat him to sleep every night for weeks. I bought him all I could to make up for the wrong I'd done. Material things have never made my son happy, he simply wanted Mom and Dad together, but I had to stick to my guns and not allow violence around my children. Violence and the drugs were the two things that kept me away from him. Our son was on punishment for months, Thanksgiving was coming around again and my family was returning.

My son had one more week of punishment. On Thanksgiving Day he asked, "Mommy can we go to Burger King?" I said, "Son we have tons of food, why Burger King?" He never spoke; he gave me the look, I need to talk look. Brett had allowed our son to have phone time that day. He had gotten a call about one of his close friends he'd gotten in trouble with, had been killed the night before. He was devastated! He told me that day as we sat in the Burger King parking lot. He stated, "Mom, if I hadn't been on punishment I would have been with them last night and you would be sad today. Mom, I'm so glad I was on punishment."

Airyka Edwards

Wow! What a statement for a fourteen year old. I grabbed him and hugged him and said, "Thank you, baby, for saying that, because I felt really bad about the longevity of your punishment. "But it would have been unfair for me to overstep dad on you punishment. The boys had gotten bored the night before and had gone out to rob a pawn shop with a toy gun, but the owner had a real gun and started shooting as the boys ran away. I prayed for the grieving family and thanked God for mine that day. It truly was a Thanksgiving Day!

I remember being so stressed out after that! Brett returned home and problems hit us again. The doctor I worked for could tell. I was still smiling every day, but she knew something wasn't quite right, so we did lunch away from the office to talk. She mentioned counseling, but Brett and I had always said we'd never allow anyone in our marriage, so that was out of the question. My nephew was working and in college by now and doing well; one less problem. Addison was so involved with school and being on the flag line. She was doing awesome while some of her friends were into boys and getting pregnant. I had to distance her from some of those friends. Being in the eighth grade and not into boys just yet made that task easier.

The doctor and I would go to Shreveport and Lake Charles often to shop. She loved to shop on her birthday and buy the girls in the office and myself everything she could to keep her mind off of birthdays. She is a beautiful woman and has never looked her age. She and I had long talks about relationships, our spirituality and the fate of the future. I could always be pretty frank with her and her with me. I asked her one day, "Why aren't you married? Don't you want a family and to be happy?" Not that she wasn't happy, but those questions lingered and she answered. She let me know she'd dated while in medical school, but soon realized "a man" per say can't give you happiness and money doesn't either. I responded, "But it sure helps! I didn't want a broke man!" (Laugh)

We talked for hours that day. As we continued our discussion she asked, "Does your husband make you happy? I mean truly give you all you need?" I sat and thought before answering, and I responded by saying, "Seriously relationships are such a responsibility! Being intimate with your spouse is such a chore at times!" She cracked up laughing and I kept talking. I told her I'm never truly happy although I love my husband dearly. My children are my joy and my pain at times, but remember earlier in the chapter "Life in Texas" there is no true happiness on this earth and should you find it, it will be only with your God. I believe that is the only true happiness in existence. As time moved on, we get orders to Missouri! We were happy to leave only because Brett would continue to be deployed if we extended our tour in Louisiana.

I was so nervous and unsure about our move. Another PCS move means a totally different place and a new life, so one day I called a very close confidant of mine, "Ms. Tunsell". I wanted to ask if she would give me some spiritual insight on upcoming events in my life. We talked and she shared ideas with me for an hour. She told me she knew that I would be working at a hospital about two minutes from our house we were going to live in. I kind of disputed that somewhat because as I shared with her I'd never worked in a hospital, nor had we planned to move off base in another town. She said, "Well, just set that on a shelf if it doesn't apply to you." We continued our conversation and she started to talk about a

Airyka Edwards

little girl running around our house! I thought maybe she, "Ms. Tunsell" sipped a little something before I called. God love her! I don't think she drinks. We both had other things on our agenda for that day so we had to end our extended conversation. I feel so refreshed and rejuvenated every time I speak with her! All I can say is she is so funny, so in touch with God and her spirituality, so sharp and so right! Needless to say she told me all these things that have now come to pass. About six months after moving to Missouri, we owned a home, we live two minutes from the hospital and Maddison has been running around our home since 2006. She gave me so much comfort to know our move was going to be okay and that we would survive, as usual. At least in Missouri Brett would teach at the chemical school house and be home more often. I had grown to love our town in Louisiana. The people were awesome. The crew God blessed me to work with at the doctor's office, "Connie and Cassandra are awesome women. We continue to keep in touch. We support our joys and our sorrows. We still call and have coffee "on the phone". I was blessed to cross paths with some of God's greatest people He created right there in Louisiana. I thank God for the developed relationships He allowed me to have. The hardest thing about leaving was telling my most precious teacher, instructor, friend and employer goodbye. I thought we'd lose what we'd developed, but every time we talk we pick right back up where we left off, talking about our God, our passion and our destiny.

Chapter Eleven

Our Transition To "Missouri"

It was mid April when the children and I packed the last of our apartment, preparing for a new transition. Brett had gone weeks before to find a place to live until we closed on the home we had chosen. The children and I drove making it safely after an eleven hour drive. My son cried half of the trip because once again he had to leave his friends of five years and his girlfriend.

Addison and I laughed a lot on the trip because the dogs' breath was so stinky and they were panting so badly. Every place we stopped to eat or let the dogs out we were laughing so hard we couldn't even order food! We tried to make the best of it. I tried comforting my son by telling him his girlfriend may come visit and we would pay for it. That was a mistake I made in life with him, trying to comfort instead of teaching and letting him know; life isn't always fair so deal with it. You're going to lose friends, family, and jobs. I guess on the flip side that is simply being a mother too, not wanting your child to hurt or feel the pain that life and life events sometimes bring us. A few days after arriving, we placed the children in school, one that housed about fourteen hundred students. They both met new friends. Me, I was busy just learning which way to turn on the main road when simply leaving or returning to the house. It took a few days to get the animals situated to their new environment. We had Lucky who was given to us by the military police in Louisiana. They picked him up one New Years Eve night after someone threw him out of a moving car. The police lived next door to us and knew we loved animals; however we were at our limit. We already had Angel a flea market mutt we got for twenty dollars and two cats Kelsey and Cinny, Addison was highly allergic to them, but loved cats! Kelsey was from the shelter and Cinny, very small, we'd picked up one year later. Addison brought her home from band practice where she had somehow ended up in her hands! Lucky was full of ticks but otherwise looked okay. Brett cleaned him up getting every tick off. I started him on preventive heart worm medicine and two weeks later he became deathly ill. I was up first around 5 A.M. to find the living room looking like someone had been murdered with blood and feces everywhere. Lucky was so weak he couldn't even walk outside. I had to carry him like an infant. He passed out outside. I rushed and got a sheet to wrap him up. By now Brett was awake. I gave him instructions to please get Lucky to the vet's off base. The final results were Lucky had a very bad case of heart worms and I triggered it by giving him the preventive medication! I felt awful! The vet, an older man with much experience called me at work and said it was going to cost us one thousand two hundred dollars, but he could probably get him better. I had my doubts being that poor Lucky was in such horrible shape! Now I knew why they threw him out.

We were "PCS'ing"; moving to Missouri and my husband stated we couldn't spend that kind of money. I cried the next day at work trying not to let anyone see the tears. The doctor I worked for at the time asked, "Airyka, why are you sad and crying?" I told her Lucky was sick and Brett doesn't want me to spend that amount on vet fees. My doctor was outraged! She said, "We will get it taken care of!" I told her, "I'm paying it whether he likes it or not!" He agreed in the first place to keep the dog, so together she and I took care of Lucky's vet fees. Funny how Brett never missed the six hundred dollars I paid out.

Arriving late in the spring and the kids had only about four weeks left of school. We spent weeks painting our new home, shampooing carpet, putting in a pool and then we hit a "house" rough spot. The septic began to seep under the house. The previous residents assured us they would have that problem fixed "per the realtor". Needless to say they didn't. We dished out almost six thousand dollars for repairs.

Then in August we received a call from Brett's mother, who was very ill. Brett was away in training for a couple of months, so I had to get Red Cross to submit a request for Brett to get out of training for two weeks. His mother's prognosis was poor. She called me the next day to tell me she had cancer. She cried and told me I'd been the best daughter-in-law ever and that she loved me very much. I think she knew she was nearing the end of her life on earth. Brett came home in two days and the next day we rushed to South Carolina. I had asked neighbors, Chirp and Emily, to help watch over the children, because we didn't really know anyone else. They are awesome people. They were there for anything the kids needed.

Airyka Edwards

Back in South Carolina my mother-in-law had her first chemotherapy treatment the Monday we arrived. She was weak, but looked great. We visited with her and her husband; we stayed a week, hoping her condition would improve. I could tell she wasn't doing as well as her sons thought she was. Sadly, the family asked my opinion and I told them to prepare for her passing soon. I had the privilege and honor to help bath her; she wanted no one else but me. I was so blessed to have the opportunity to give back a fraction of what she had done for me. We had to leave that Friday morning to return to Missouri, to check on our children and the house. The ride home was the longest I'd ever taken. My husband was quiet and his brother kept calling to see if he should fly out to see their mother. I told him if he wanted to see her alive he should go as fast as he could. Brett and I were both mentally exhausted!

As though that wasn't enough God showed me as plain as day a violent event was going to happen in our family. At first I told Brett, "Oh my goodness, I'm having a bad premonition!" When I remembered, "warning comes before destruction" I told my husband that in a few weeks someone, a male, in our family was going to have a horrific encounter. He stated, "Oh it's probably my brother going to have another heart attack." My brother-in-law had already survived a Quadruple bypass, a stroke and other health problems. I told Brett, "No honey, it's in my family, not yours. As soon as we arrived back in Missouri I hurriedly told my son what I had been shown, "he was so scared!" I told him to just drive to school and come straight home every day and he did just that for almost a month.

No Longer Bound

Sadly, we got a call the day after arriving home saying to hurry and fly back my mother-in-law was in the hospital not expected to live. I wasn't surprised. We flew back to Carolina the next day leaving the kids once again. We left them money and went grocery shopping for food that was about all we had time to do. My mother-in-law passed away about one hour before we arrived at the airport. I was devastated! My poor husband and his brother were just lost, as any of us would be after losing a parent that was so beloved.

We stayed, to bury her, the following Thursday. More pain and hurt for our family once again. For days I didn't know how to tell my husband I was so sorry he'd lost his mother. I finally got the words out on the day of her funeral as I sobbed my eyes out. I told him I shared his pain and his grief. While there for a few more days I received a call from my mother. I thought she was calling to comfort or say, "I'm sorry for your loss", but no, that was not the case. She called to ask me to wire her fifty dollars to help her buy a dress. I said," Mom I'm here burying my mother-in-law I can't do that." She stated, "Well can you just find a store right quick and send it to me?" I wanted to yell so bad and say did you hear me, I'm grieving! I thought why even try? My mother could care less; it was once again all about her. I said, "Mom I have to go "and I hung the phone up. The Lord laid it on my heart before leaving Germany to pay all of my mother's debt off when I returned to the states. She had loans from several companies. My sister told me all her money was going to pay loan companies. I never asked what she did with all the money she acquired from those companies. God simply told me what to do and I did it.

Airyka Edwards

We buried Jan Edwards on September 2nd. She would have turned seventy years old on September 17th that year. She and her husband along with my brother-in-law all had tickets to fly to Missouri to celebrate her birthday here with us. We left there on Saturday, heading back to Missouri and we arrived home safely, thank God.

Early one morning around 5 A.M, I received a call from my niece, Sabrina. She was screaming and crying! I could hardly understand her. "Auntie, Auntie!" she yelled. She was trying to tell me my baby brother, Lanardo had been shot the night before at his apartment! It was approximately mid October. I remember while talking with my niece I began to wail pretty badly. My son heard me and he came running in my room and asked, "Mom, Mom what happened? Why are you crying Mommy?" I hung the phone up and told my son, "Your Uncle Lanardo has been shot! We don't know his status. He was still in surgery from last night!" My son held me and began to pat me on the back trying all he could to console me. Soon minutes later he said, "Mom I'm sorry this happened to your brother, but I'm so glad this is over!" I looked at him and said, "Glad what is over son?" He said, "Mom, remember a few weeks ago you said something really bad was going to happen to someone in our family, a male?" I said, "Yes!" He said, "Mom I've been so scared that it was me and that you were going to be hurt if something happened to me. Mom, I'm so happy this is over!" I said, "Baby I am too and I'm sorry if I scared you, but I didn't know, I just didn't know who it was."

My brother is still alive, but is paralyzed from his waist down. He is very angry for the cards life has dealt him. As one of my patients once told me, "Honey God already had this planned. He just didn't

No Longer Bound

clue me in until it was time." She was speaking of her previous cancer she had survived, so no matter how good of a person my brother was, God had his life planned, he just didn't clue any of us in until October! My brother already had it pretty rough in life, just as the rest of us had, we were doing what we had to do to survive. He never finished school. He would do odd jobs to gather money to help our mother. I vividly remember some hot, sweaty summers my brother would go out early in the morning to mow grass for people for five to ten dollars a yard and come home late in the evening hungry, tired and very hot. He would give our mother every dime he'd made. I recall one day he was so hungry and tired he asked my mother if he could have a plate of food. She obliged him and fixed him a nice size plate piled with food and made him eat outside under the house. I never knew why my mom treated my brother and me so bad sometimes. I began to ask questions, years later to simply find she seemed to hate us at times because of our "father's sins"! I'm sure she often wondered why my brother's dad, "Mr. Lanardo Blue", never married her. He was "one step dad" I didn't mind being around. He worked and brought my mother the check home. He also bought food for us. I remember one particular time he made us a homemade chocolate cake from scratch! That man could cook! We always felt safe when "Mr. Blue" was around. I remember my mother would make him hide if someone else came by the house, woman or man. It seemed she really liked Mr. Blue, but was ashamed to be seen with him. He really loved my mother, but he also loved his wife back in Utica, Mississippi too! Yes he was married all those years and no one in our family knew until the day he died, three weeks after my father passed away.

Airyka Edwards

Mr. Blue and my mother had two children together as far as we know. I often regretted not going to Mr. Blue's funeral, but my husband would not allow me to because he knew I was still grieving everyday over losing my dad. I did get to visit with Mr. Blue the week I buried my dad. I had asked around town and searched until I found his house. We had the best visit that day. He asked me to go to the store and get him a soda and one for his daughter I had never met. I went to the store and bought him a case of soda and gave him twenty dollars for any extras he needed. That was one man I thanked God for! He never touched any of us girls in any inappropriate way. I truly loved him.

I'm sure by now you're saying, "Gees' girl what other family secrets do you have?" Let me just tell you this book is merely an edited version of my life; a quarter of a quarter fraction, but not a "tell all "However, I do have a lot to tell, but could never get it all in one book.

As time flew by it was graduation time for our son. I'd landed a job at St. Mary's Hospital, and Brett was retiring. We'd purchased our first home together and had real civilian bills, including paying taxes I never knew existed! Stress was starting to set in for us all! Brett was scrambling wondering what he would do; how will he handle life without the military. I was working in Same Day Surgery at the time. A few weeks later a beautiful young lady met me at the stairs one morning coming out of my son's room as I came out of mine! Panic set in! I was hoping she broke in and had not been let in and slept in my son's room. All she could say was, "It's not what you think, Ma'am." She saw the look on my face! I said, "Well what is it then?" She proceeded to grab her purse out

No Longer Bound

of my son's room and lunged out the front door! I informed Brett about what was going on.

Days later I pulled up in my truck from work, got out and she's in the driveway talking to my son. She said, "Hello Ma'am." I looked at her and simply asked, "Are you on birth control?" She answered in disgust, "Well, yes Ma'am, I'm on the Depo shot." I'd been working in OB/GYN for almost five years and knew nothing is a guarantee. She looked as I kept walking with a "yeah right" look on my face as I walked in to the house! We didn't see her for a few months after that.

In the months we didn't see her, she'd been incarcerated. She took ill while behind bars for a DUI to later find out she was pregnant! I'd remembered a week prior my son stated, "Mom, I need to talk with you." Our family always sat together at the dinner table every evening around 6 P.M. unless you were dead or at some type of school function you were not excused. We had dinner as a family, no TV and no electronics were allowed at the dinner table. "My rule" and it still exist today. Before my son could build up the nerve to tell anything about their situation, the jail attendant called the young lady's grandmother to inform her that her granddaughter was pregnant. The grandmother called all departments at the hospital to find me and after doing so told me her granddaughter was pregnant by our son! I remember getting sick to my stomach and having to leave out of surgery for a few minutes to catch fresh air and throw up! I had to go home that evening to tell Brett. He went ballistic! "What the double hockey sticks was he thinking?" Brett stated.

Airyka Edwards

Reality hit us all a few days later after we had calmed down and accepted it. The deed was done. We made it mandatory our son had to finish school. Once the flames died down, the shouting, the numbness and the final shock wore off a bit we sat down to discuss his future. Seriously we'd taught him if he ever made the choice to do something of the sort with a girl to please use protection. The tension in our house was as thick as a 2 x 4!

Brett and I were once again not getting along. He wanted to do so many things to the house for improvements, so we weren't allowed any vacation. He took the checkbook from me and said I was spending too much money! Which I was not guilty of at the time. That same year his ex-wife took us back to court for more child support, which she had every right to do and she won. My family was coming down for our son's graduation. We had about nineteen people coming, including the children's grandmother from Louisiana. She was in a wheel chair, but still came. I also had planned a retirement party for Brett the next day after the graduation. Brett thought I was planning a big barbeque for my son's graduation, but all my family knew for months it was for Brett. I had some of his closest friends from the Military, to come over because they wanted to present him with a gift from the "The Dragon Soldier"; their platoon had all pitched in and had a photo made, framed and matted for him. My family had all gotten him gift cards because they knew Brett was always working on something around the house. I remember at the graduation everyone stood to yell and clap for our son. We were so proud of him, but Brett sat there! I was appalled that he would do that to the kid he told years before he was his father and would take care of him and stick by him. I was truly ashamed he did such a thing.

The next day it was so hot and I had run around cooking all night to ensure we had mega amounts of everything for his retirement party. Around 10 A.M. that morning I was in the kitchen putting final touches on everything making salad mix and so forth, while he was behind me like a devil taunting me saying "I don't know why you would plan something so big as hot as it is outside!" I tried to keep my composure with everything I had. I held it together as the children's grandmother sat and looked on while we were talking. I tried not to cry or make any facial expressions at all. My level of stress that day was on a scale from one to ten was one hundred fifty! As I completed the salad I went outside to ask everyone to gather the rest of the family and friends who had come including military friends who had just arrived. I gave my son permission to leave that day after his buddies came to get him. Brett stated, "The kid can't even stay for his own party. He has to run the streets!" I said nothing. Minutes later we gathered outside with over thirty one people singing and shouting, "Happy retirement to SFC Brett Edwards!" Yes, he looked at me with shame! He couldn't believe all this was for him! I had special ordered a humongous cake which I had hid in the formal dining room. Food galore! Baby back ribs, shrimp, pork steaks, brisket, brats, chicken, potato salad, green salad, homemade macaroni and cheese, red beans and rice with Louisiana sausage in it, corn on the cob and much more, Brett had horse shoes set up to play, volleyball nets, card games, dart board and so many other activities. Everyone had a blast. We rode our four-wheeler; my family, namely my sisters hadn't ever been on anything like that! My sister's hair flew back for the first time in history! She loved it! The festivities went on until around 6 or 7 P.M. which by then I was exhausted and hurt. My friend, Cory tried to take me upstairs

Airyka Edwards

to comfort me and I remember I just broke! The tears flowed and my burden of so much was like ripping the scab off of a sore and pouring salt in the wound! That's a fraction of my pain and hurt just that day! Brett came upstairs to pretend he cared and I just told him to leave me alone. I survived the day by the pure grace of God. The next day everyone was so tired and just kind of laid around the house, so later that day it was my time. I told my sister I'm going to my truck and taking Brett to talk. I also told her if she heard a shot don't come see, just call 911. I took my twenty-two caliber pistol with me to the truck I had had enough! I was done being sad. I was mad; mad at myself for allowing my husband to have treated me like this for so long. I had "allowed" this, however by the choices I made. I could have nipped it in the bud from the get go years before when he would pull his control stunts and cards, but I turned my head instead of facing the problem. I chose to act as if it didn't happen. I smiled and never let on to anyone, except my sister and my friend Cory, and they only knew a tiny bit of what was really happening. I felt like a Stepford wife, at times. Everyone thought we were the model couple. He got to look like the sainted father, husband, and uncle while the kids sometimes thought Mom is just being ugly not talking to Dad. Remember I vowed never to allow any violence or arguments around my children until the day they moved out.

Brett and I had a three hour discussion in the truck that night. He apologized as usual and asked me to please help him get better. Those were always his famous words. I wasn't buying it this time. I let him know things had to change. We needed counseling and he needed Prozac!

No Longer Bound

A month passed and things were great, until he ran out of medicine. I made him another doctor appointment. He stated he thought he calmed down some and to give him a break. Well, he was on terminal leave for a few months, which are the final days off before your exit from the military. It gives you time to transition to civilian life, house, taxes, job, and stress! Some guys do well. Some can't or simply don't make the transition. With twenty some odd years in the military you pretty much know where your next check and meal is coming from, you're okay. You wear the same uniform just clean every day, spit shine your shoes and have a perfect haircut. Those habits are good for some and very hard to break, for others. Our new transition was not going too well.

November came around and our granddaughter was due Thanksgiving Day. We all went to Texas to visit my sister and her family that year. My son was told by Brett he needed to stay home just in case his child was born, we had a very odd visit that year in Texas. We arrived on Wednesday evening, sat around and talked until about 11 P.M. I finally told Brett, Addison and I were hungry, so we left to go get food. We were even unsure where we were to sleep that night. We thought we were staying at one of my niece's house, because we had been invited, only to be told by my sister we were staying at her house. That was so uncomfortable, because my sister's husband still owed my husband money, from a deal they struck up before we left for Germany. My brother-in-law bought my husband's truck, they signed an agreement, my husband took his word, and they shook hands. Unfortunately my husband was never paid for his truck and I kindly asked him to please not say anything about it on this trip. Brett respected my

105

wishes. Early Friday morning after Thanksgiving, we departed and drove back to Missouri.

Maddison was born by c-section, so we got to be there the following Monday. Brett and our son got to see and hold her first; I was working at a company giving flu shots. My Director took up my slack and I drove to the hospital as soon as my son called and said, "She's here Mom, she's here!" Oh wow, all the anger left that day when we all got to hold our little princess for the first time. Maddison and her mother got to come home with us for a couple weeks. Shortly after, her mother took her out of state for almost a month. It was after New Year's when we saw her again.

Maddison's mother had a troubled past. After she returned back to town we got to visit with her. My goodness, Maddison had grown and she had gained a lot of weight! She was beautiful! We were often sad when she wasn't around. She quickly became the light that brightens our lives and boy did we need it! I won't elaborate too much out of respect for the privacy of Maddison's mother's family. They are awesome people, very loving, generous and always willing to lend a helping hand to try to make life easier for us all.

At ten weeks old, Maddison was in our custody as a ward through the state. That year was such a horrific year. By February 2007 Missouri had a bad ice storm that lasted for weeks, just about everyone lost power in their homes, rich and poor. I recall having to put our children in a hotel for almost a week because our house was so cold. Maddison's mother called to come over for shelter, but we had no heat. We put them both in a hotel for a couple of nights. When I went to the office to pay for another night the

No Longer Bound

manager said, "No, she had to leave!" I said, "Why, sir they have no heat?" He said she'd had a loud party and he could not tolerate that at his hotel.

My husband went on a mission to find a generator. He found two at Lowes to get his family heat. He also remembered he had an old kerosene heater that he had from his parents from when he was a child. We put all our animals upstairs in our bedroom with the heater; two dogs and two cats. We got the generator going and functioned as well as could be expected! At the time I had just started working in Wellness. The other nurse in that department and I had been summoned to work the Civic Center in our town that had been turned into the local shelter. It was the largest facility the community had to house over four hundred people. They slept on cots. We had some people in isolation due to chronic illnesses, pregnant women in their last trimester, babies crying just wanting to be held, people in wheel chairs and oxygen all around the walls. It was one of the most distressing sights I'd ever seen. I took my mind back to what shelters must had been like during hurricane Katrina and this was merely a fraction of what those people must have endured!

We administered over-the-counter medicines. Red Cross and Job Corps people were there helping around the clock, cleaning bedding, bathrooms, and making Wal-Mart runs. Our local hospital supplied and donated free flu shots, medicines, food and so much more. The hospital ER staff was overwhelmed with people just needing simple medical care, but had nothing at home and had come there for help. Some of us hospital workers stayed at work morning and night before we'd leave to go home. Through it all, our community pulled together like it was a normal day to pitch in and help each other. Approximately two weeks later, the electricity came back on. God had really blessed us because we'd just filled three of our freezers full of meat and we lost nothing compared to what our community had encountered. We managed to put our lives back together, just as a new problem arose.....

What to do with a ten week old granddaughter while we work? My psychological condition at this point was crazy! Our daughter, Addison was a junior in school and working at a daycare where she was also interning. She knew a few mothers of her friends who stayed home and didn't work. Addison made calls and by the next day she had found us a sitter until we could get her into daycare. There were ladies from work who also knew others who would help, Connie, Polly Renee, and Kat. These ladies were "our life savers" for weeks. We thanked God each day for having such wonderful people in our lives. Our daughter was also willing to do whatever she could. She heard me one night over into the early morning standing over Maddison's crib, just crying. I was so tired and Maddison was colicky and fussy. Addison came in and said, "Mommy just lie down for awhile, I'll get her for now." I just hugged her and thanked her for everything, but made her go back to bed; this wasn't her fight or her child!

By now you are wondering where the child's father is. He worked nights at the factory up the street and didn't get off until 4:30 A.M. I remember by the second week of what I thought was my "last mental trimester " when he came home one morning, I was up just sitting downstairs. He sat down and began to talk. His exact words were, "Mom, I'm so sorry for putting you and Dad through this. I wish I could change it or help. Mom, I can't even

108

No Longer Bound

help myself let alone you guys." I looked at him with hurt and sadness and said, "Son it will get better. God will lighten the load." I told him how much I appreciated the courage it took to say the words and apologize. That meant more than he will ever know. We hugged and moved on.

Time seemed to move slow, but don't ever say what you "can't" do. I thought I would lose my mind before it was all said and done. Oh but for the love of God! My pastor always said, "God can! God will!" ALL I had at that time was my faith to hold on to and it was being weakened by my day to day life. One minute I would think things are looking up the next minute you wonder, "Where is my God?" We go through so many unnecessary trials, I say unnecessary because God will help if we ask. Usually we try to fix it ourselves when in reality we need to leave ourselves alone, let yourself be.......let yourself be faithful.....let yourself be prayerful..... "*Let this mind be in you, which was also in Christ Jesus" Philippians 2:5 KJV* Remember God already has our future planned. He just doesn't clue us in until it's time, whether it be a job, cancer or a child. Whether it is good in our eyes or bad, leave yourself alone. If we could fix ourselves we wouldn't need God. God said in Genesis 1 KJV so many times "*Let there be.....*" God made man, animals, and the world in six days just by saying, "*Let there be...*" and on the seventh day He rested. Imagine what you and I could do if we would simply, let go and let God. "When God is all you have, really that's all you need!

Maddison was a sickly little girl. I remember the day DFS (Department of Family Services) called and wanted us to meet them at our home. They asked us if we would like to have Maddison or if we wanted her to go to foster care. Well I immediately said,

109

Airyka Edwards

"She can go to foster Care and we will see her on weekends and buy her what she needs." I was dead serious. My thoughts were, our last one is about to graduate and we didn't want to begin any new endeavors. Boy was I wrong! My husband spoke up and said, "No grandchild of ours is going to foster care! It's not the child's fault!" Her mother's sides of the family were mostly up in age and could not properly care for a new child. But they did help financially.

I didn't care! All I could think of was getting up fixing bottles and changing diapers! I was not ready! I looked at Brett and said, "Are you going to get up and fix bottles when she is hungry, change her diapers, take her to the doctors when she is sick or throw it all on me?" He looked at me and said, "Yes Dear I will help with it all." I must say he did not lie. He has been an awesome "Papa" to her. Those two have a closeness that no one could interfere with. He truly has not missed a beat. As I said animals and children, he loves.

Time flew by and we were preparing for our daughter to graduate. She was seventeen years old and had gone to college a year by the time she graduated from her senior year in high school. She wanted to drop out of dance. I was okay with that, but told her she had to do something else constructive to preoccupy her time, so night classes it was. I was really happy to see my children walk across the stage and graduate from high school. It was an achievement their biological father said I couldn't do! I can do "all" things through Christ that strengthened me and so can you!

After graduation she moved out and my son had already moved on, so for a few months we had the house to ourselves with the little one. I'd tried to make life easier and better for us. I bought a lot of magazines on "cooking for two". I was trying new recipes and cooking less food. I was used to cooking a lot. I made my children breakfast every morning until the day my children turned eighteen.

Brett and I seemed to be relating better. He saw the changes I was trying to make. Maddison had adjusted to life very well as far as daily routine. That sweet little life as we knew it was short lived! Addison moved back home. Her boyfriend had messed things up with her roommate by taking over her own house and got mouthy about it. A few months down the road she quit her daycare job. She had worked there almost five years from her freshman year to after she graduated, so she was jobless and partying with friends. I nailed down a harder curfew and for the most part she complied. When she didn't I was on the stairs sitting waiting on her when she came in. My children knew when I said be home I meant it! She was going down the wrong road and not walking too straight on it either. By March 2010 she was not working at all. I signed her up for Max Job Camps in St. Louis. She was mortified! I felt I had to get her away from her boyfriend and others who weren't good for her. She and her boyfriend made a trip to Texas before going to camp where she would work all summer. I suppose while she was on her trip they made a pit stop to sleep, because the end of June the camp director sent her home. She was throwing up and very ill. One thing I knew for sure, she wasn't Bulimic or Anorexic because she was losing no food she didn't have to. She texted to tell me she was pregnant! I told her not to play with me like that, but she wasn't. I told her I wanted nothing to do with her! I had always taken her to the base for her birth control and she

Airyka Edwards

had been on it for years before dating. She had some pretty bad monthly cycles so her doctor saw fit to try and regulate those with birth control. I recall three months before she left for Texas, I told her she was of age to go get her own birth control, I'd made her several appointments. She refused making several excuses.

She had no idea that before she left for her job in St. Louis I had rented myself an apartment! Everything that happened with the kids, Brett blamed me. We were back to square one! I was so tired of the same old same old after almost fifteen years. I'd had enough. I told him I was filing for a divorce! I moved out one Wednesday while he was at work. I did have the courtesy to call and tell him so he'd know before he got home. I was done! Tired of being hurt, tired of pain, tired of coming home from work, not knowing what mood he would be in, and tired of not talking for months. I have a hidden demon that I only use when someone has really upset or hurt me. If I care enough to allow you in my life, my heart, and my family and if you deceive or cross me in any negative way, I will not talk to you for weeks, I would amputate you from my life for months or even years! At this time I hadn't spoken to my husband in four months. I would come home from work and cook, clean, spend a little time with Maddison, shower and go to bed. My husband had moved out of the bedroom months prior.

What you think you want is not always what God has planned! Now mind you Brett hadn't beaten me, nor had he cheated on me to my knowledge. I moved out completely and started my life over in a two bedroom apartment across town. I began to think finally I have peace of mind; no one to tell me not to spend money, what to spend, nor no one to tease me about retiring to bed early in the evenings. I was awake most mornings around 4

112

No Longer Bound

to 4:30 A.M. due to my job and the early mornings it required. I was finally on my own again after fifteen years. Maddison seemed to be happy with her new room, but every night she wanted her Papa, who had cradled her since birth. We shared her on Wednesday and every other weekend. I called a few of my family members to alert them of what had transpired in my life. They were astonished, responding with, "Oh my Auntie", "Oh my Airyka" "Sis what happened?" "We never knew you guys ever had any problems." I proceeded first of all to let them know I never had the opportunity to tell anyone my problems, because I was everyone's ear. I was the rational one to make sense for them with all their problems. I was the problem solver in my family for years. No one really ever stopped to ask, "How are you Airyka? How are you guys dealing with your new move, your new home state, new jobs, retirement, new addition to the family and by the time I left Brett, we'd had another granddaughter. Brett was furious over the fact that our son had two children and wasn't married. Addison was pregnant but it was my fault somehow. No one once asked, "How is everything going for your family Airyka?" except for my niece Sabrina and my sister Ranne. I have been blessed and have always enjoyed helping others with their problems, so I wasn't complaining.

As soon as the news reached over half of my siblings I started receiving calls, "Hey, girl how is everything?" My oldest sister all of a sudden called to tell me she was going to send me some fish; funny how I never received it, but I just let her know, "Sweetheart, I know why you called and it sure wasn't for the fish! Yes, Brett and I are not together at this time." I asked another one of my sisters to loan me some money until I got settled. She gave it to

113

Airyka Edwards

me and I just knew after all I had done for her that five hundred dollars was going to be on the house! Never hold your breath when family is involved! Trust me I paid it back and then some with having to send this and that to her as if I had money growing on trees. I felt guilty so anything (they) asked for, I've always sent it.

I tried coping with all this. I even went to my lawyer and paid him a lump sum from monies I'd taken from our joint account before I left. I told my lawyer to rush it so I wouldn't change my mind. The sweetest thing ever doing this whole ordeal our family lawyer, Bob, refused to take my case. He stated, "Airyka, I'm too close to the family to do that." He let me know he cared about Brett and I both and would not side with either of us in this situation. However, he did try to help me. He walked me down the street to a close friend of his that I hadn't met before. I instructed him with the same message, to hurry the procedure please so I don't change my mind! He said, "I will do my best, Airyka" During this time of living away from my husband, did I miss him? Yes! I still loved him very much!

Although we hadn't had any physical contact for four to five months, I did say goodnight every night and gave him a kiss each night. I never said I hated him or didn't want to be with him, I left because I hated the way he treated me and blamed me for everything. We both even went on a date with a different partner. I thought just maybe this would help me get over him and he thought the same. However, neither one of us knew God's plan. He just simply gave us a break.

Memorial Day weekend was when I moved out. I had always told him and anyone else that cared to know, "I married because I wanted a man not because I needed a man." I made that clear several times to him and others. I also made him aware that I do not believe in forever nor will I ever believe in forever, when it comes to a man, marriage, friendship or any tangible or non-tangible person or thing. I've had a lot of friends to deceive me, hurt me and turn on me. "No –Thing" last forever. My eternity is with one person and that is my God, my faith is in one person. Again I say that is my God.

After a few weeks I still continued praying and going to church. I missed one Sunday and my pastor emailed me to ask why because I had been so faithful. I sadly told him I was finishing my move. I explained to him I'd left my husband and had moved out of our home. He was troubled and saddened by the news and apologized for not realizing I had problems. I explained to him I was a private person and really never had anyone to talk to so I just dealt with my situations alone as I had always done. He and his wife reached out to me at church with many hugs and prayers. They continued to pray for me as always, that's just who they are. They did not try to force me to talk and tell them anything. They had always said, Sis Airyka, we are here if you need us, I knew in my heart they meant every word and still do, to this day.

God began to deal with me through his word. Every time I would go to church it's like a Rhema! A "fresh word from the Lord" every time I step foot in my church. God began to have me focus more on him now that I had more time to do so. I began to be reminded, "I stood before God and witnesses in his holy sanctuary and said, "I do. From this day forward, for better, for WORSE, for richer, for poorer, in sickness and in health, to love and to cherish, till death do us part." And now I've left the man I said God gave me.

Airyka Edwards

It's funny how we appreciate our spouse and God when all is going well, but when the going gets tough we walk away. I left way before I physically left. At my apartment I had some nice quiet days and nights, so I went to God and just asked Him to take over my life, my mind, and my heart. I asked God to lead me and to allow His will to be done not what I wanted, but if it was meant for me to be with my husband to fix everything that was wrong.

I never took in consideration that my husband was encountering his own fire! He confided in me that he was dealing with depression and separation anxiety from the Military. My husband is one of the smartest, most intelligent men I know, but even the strongest man with those top virtues; he couldn't stop "PTSD" Post Traumatic Stress Disorder. Even the strong need strength to survive. Within two years my husband lost his mother to cancer, his only brother had a Stroke and Heart attack, and we had his children and my children graduating on the same day. His stress was at an all time high! But God brought him out alright!

Brett and I would have several talks about us, our marriage and more. Some were good talks, some turned into verbal fights, but when asked if I still loved him I had to be truthful, Yes! I still loved my husband.

When love is real, it doesn't fade overnight. I was fighting, it seemed, a losing battle. I wanted my husband to be nice to me, not so verbal aggressive. I wanted him to stop buying so many "man" toys, because most of our fights were over money and the children. I remember our last fight before I left. I'd gone out of state for work for a couple of weeks and I used the bank card to buy me a new pair of nursing shoes and a seventeen dollar pair of jeans on sale, that was sixty dollars. I got home that Friday and was met at the door about forty two dollars that I had spent. Brett also instructed me to terminate our housekeeper of five years. I thought we were going bankrupt, but in two weeks he had a Bobcat and trailer for it sitting outside with a new one ton truck he purchased. I was livid!

I took a break while living on my own to go to Mississippi for the Fourth of July. I hadn't been home in five years and just wanted to spend some time with my family, some had come home as well to see my mother. I think I saw my mother maybe for five minutes; she really didn't want to be bothered. However I went to my dad's grave for comfort. I sat there and talked to him telling him what had transpired in my life. I told him if heaven and God is real; show me, by fixing my marriage and making it right, not just back together. I wanted some happiness rather contentment at this point would have been nice, just for once, without having to keep my guard up and ready to fight and defend all the time. I was beginning to think life doesn't offer beauty, peace, or sanity for me.

We had a wonderful visit with my family that year. As we drove back to Missouri on Sunday morning my son and Maddison both slept just about all the way home. I prayed a lot that day. I returned to work on Monday with all smiles and a heavy heart.

I woke up Tuesday morning with a sick feeling about my life (God was still working) and the choices I'd made I thought "Oh my goodness" what have I done? I stepped out of your will and I have sinned. Besides all that, my husband had repeatedly told me, "I can't believe you left me!" He was in shock and so was I! That

Airyka Edwards

same day I called Brett to inform him I was coming by the house to discuss the divorce proceedings, because I'd spoken to my lawyer.

I had to teach a CRP class that same evening at a factory. I took Maddison over to see Brett for a few days, boy was she happy! She missed her Papa. I stopped by the house around 5 P.M., my daughter and her boyfriend were also over visiting. Brett and I were out in the garage talking and I began to tell him what I was asking for in the divorce. I don't think he heard a word I said for about fifteen minutes. He was working on an air conditioner on one of the vehicles. I asked him if he'd listened to me. He sat there and said so sweet, "Dear, I don't want a divorce." For the first time in weeks, I allowed God to let my hardened heart go soft. I said, "Neither do I, but I can't live like this anymore." He looked at me with true sincerity and said, "I'll agree to counseling, meds, I'll do whatever it takes." I heard something in his voice I'd never heard before. I heard God helping and healing us. I didn't have a lot of time that evening, because I had to work, so we agreed to talk more the next day.

As we hugged in the garage our daughter and her boyfriend (whom has sense cleaned his life up and I'm so proud of him) had gone to their car, we looked up to see this huge smile on her face. She knew we were going to be fine. I rushed off to work with a smile on my face, too! The next day I went to my apartment after work and called Brett to come over so we could talk. Earlier that morning I called my lawyer to tell him I didn't want to proceed. He asked of course, "Are you sure?" I replied, "Yes I'm sure after losing twelve pounds and a lot of prayers. Yes I'm sure!" Brett came over that evening and we talked for awhile. I told him I had a confession and he said so did he. I said, "Honey, I went out on

No Longer Bound

two dates and I didn't enjoy myself. I wish the whole time it was you across the table eating with me." He said, "Well, I went out on a date too and I hated it!" I asked why. He stated, "She didn't like onions and she doesn't eat seafood!" We both laughed. I said, "Well, one of my dates was allergic to shell fish!" We both cracked up laughing, because our favorite food is seafood and we eat onions with almost every meal! I told him my other date wanted to wine and dine me, take me to Paris, Mexico and other places. I was proud to inform him that, "There's really nowhere you can take me that my husband hasn't already taken me." I let that gentleman know I wasn't totally deprived. My husband and I talked for hours and he asked me to please get started on our counseling.

I called the next day. We took it slow. We went to all of our sessions and we soaked up all we could. By the fourth session our counselor asked us both a question. She asked me to tell everything I wanted Brett to improve in or change and she asked Brett the same. She gave both of us a few minutes to gather our thoughts. As we sat in her office and the hour glass sifted away she proceeded, "Okay Airyka, you go first. How or what do you expect from Brett?" I said, "I'd like to have my own money without having to explain where I spent every dime. I'd like Brett and me to have a day twice a month just for us, not the kids or grandkids, "just us"." He said, "Okay" and we worked out formalities on my allowance.

Now it was Brett's turn. She asked, "Okay Brett, what or how would you like to see Airyka improve?" He looked at me then he looked at her and he said, "Ma'am she's a great wife, there's really nothing she could improve in." The counselor asked, those

Airyka Edwards

months she wasn't talking to you did she do what she was suppose to as a wife? He said, "Yes ma'am she did everything. She cooked, cleaned, did laundry, took care of the granddaughter she would lay my towel out for my shower and kiss me goodnight." The counselor asked "Has she ever withheld any other wifely duties from you? "Well, ma'am when she's upset or mad." I wasn't brave enough to turn over and ask. [Laugh]

Brett said, "She's a really good wife, it wasn't her it was me!" That statement brought tears and I sat there and cried. The counselor asked, "Airyka, why are you crying?" I said, "Because he's never told me I was a good wife." He's really never praised me at all, but that was just Brett. He would say thank you for a great dinner or something I cooked or yeah that dress looks nice on you and that was the extent of praise. So for him to say that it was so fulfilling, for me it was like a load being lifted, knowing how you are viewed by the other person is so important.

I don't want to bore you with other details, but that was our mending point; our first time coming together to agree on things. I've always agreed with him, but it was his presentation of it all! Brett learned that if he would think before he spoke he could probably reword some things. The way a person delivers their message, their statements makes a huge difference in the way the other party responds or accepts what was initially presented. I learned to forgive easier and faster when situations are presented to me in a respectable fashion, not verbally aggressive or with abrasive language. "Oh what needless pain we bear" as the old hymn song goes.

No Longer Bound

So my testimony through all those years is, I had lots of laughter, love and a lot of pain. My strength was always there, but at times, God took and shook my faith. I have it all back now with more discernment and clarity. I had to evaluate the choices I'd made in life and allow God to enhance my life through those choices. I was not going to allow Brett or anyone else in life to take or break the woman I'd become. I had to search and adjust myself. I didn't know how I felt until I spoke the truth. My truth was I loved my husband, but I wasn't going to live out a lie. We weren't happy. When you get tired of being tired, that's when you get power back in your life; your power is your voice. Brett couldn't fix what he didn't know was wrong. He had to gain and obtain the knowledge and strength to hear, see and accept his wrong. He didn't just "man up" he gave up! He gave up to God! Yes, today my husband is baptized in Jesus name! He gave his life to the Lord and he is saved today!(and he is still a work in progress)Laugh.

It is an important lesson; just think what if I had totally thrown in the towel and given up on my marriage? What if I'd never asked God to intervene and help us? A friend of mine said once "People go into marriage thinking if it doesn't work out I will just get a divorce. Instead of getting married "knowing" divorce is not an option. Basically divorce is too easily accepted too readily. Marriage is a Holy covenant you take before God and should be treasured as such." Stated by a friend of mine.

I remember telling Brett when we got married, he asked about adopting my children my response was, "Let's give this marriage a year and if things work out well we'll talk about adoption. If not let's agree to go our separate ways with what we came into the marriage with." I was so wrong from the start. I should have

Airyka Edwards

gone into this believing and knowing God is going to help us and be with us every step of the way. Instead I came in with a plan (B). All that to say is, yes my husband was ruthless at times and remember I was no saint! but that's when we should pray for our spouse. We pray for them to see God in us and before long, you will walk together as God intended you to, as one, not divided. I truly thank God for my "saved husband" today! He has been a wonderful provider for our family and he is a good husband. He is now aware and conscious of the things he says to me and the way he speaks to me. As the saying goes, "A family that prays together stays together." I'm thankful to God I didn't give up on him.

I moved back into our home after being gone for "forty days and forty nights". I've often said that has to count for something. Jesus fasted for "forty days and forty nights". I had to find a smile in that somewhere. [Laugh]

I now go outside to help my husband in the yard, before he would ask and my response was, "I didn't ask for "five acres"! I do appreciate him trying to make our surroundings beautiful. I also found the courage to apologize to him after all those years of not helping him. I thank God today we walk hand and hand as husband and wife, not as man and woman. I ask that you not judge me on my behavior. Yes I've gone through a lot in my life, but I honor my husband. I treat him the way God intended me to treat my spouse. "Let you that are without sin cast the first stone....." I truly thank God for this journey of marriage; the troubles are just a part of it. Today my husband is the very epitome of a real man and I'm grateful!

No Longer Bound

Many of us encounter disagreements, pain and hurtful things in a marriage, but it's not an excuse to walk away. I had to learn that the hard way. Remember this, if nothing else: *"Trust in the "Lord" with all thine heart and lean "not" unto thine own understanding"* Proverbs 3:5 KJV **v.6** *"In all thy ways acknowledge him and he shall direct thy paths."* **v. 12** *"For whom the Lord loveth he correcteth; even as a father the son in whom he delighteth."* **The Lord had to "set me straight". He had to correct me and deal with me, because he loves me and you!**

Chapter Twelve

My Angels

My Children--Their Demons—My Pain

I started my journey with my children May 1988 and June 1990. There are so many people out there in the world who have never been blessed to conceive children and have the experience of giving birth. I was thankful to God for choosing me! I became a single parent weeks after having my daughter. So with a two year old and a three week old, I started my life together with my babies. One thing always stuck in my mind. My mother said quite often, "If you have those babies, take care of them." I had to accept my choices I'd made in life to be a mother without a husband. My children were my angels. They were my stability and they forced me to hold things together whether I wanted to or not.

I remember our first Christmas together, I had to work and my daughter was six months old and my son was two and a half. I got off work around 2 P.M. and we were invited to my friends, Sherrie's mother's house for Christmas dinner. Her family was thrilled we joined them that day.

No Longer Bound

Around 6 P.M. we went home to our cozy little townhouse. I remember I had a tree someone had given me. I had a glass table (frame) with four chairs, but no glass on the table just a large hole where the glass was suppose to be. I'd rented a living room set and a queen bed for me to sleep in. I had to pay forty dollars every two weeks, but I paid it off within a year.

I bathed my children that night and later, I showered, put them to bed and passed out, I was so tired. I remember sleeping with my radio on every night when I got my own place. I heard the radio playing a Christmas song! Oh my! I jumped up at midnight and woke the children apologizing to them that I'd forgotten to let them open their few gifts I'd managed to get them. My sweet son said, "Mommy, its ok. You worked today. You were tired, really tired." That brought tears to my eyes. He was the sweetest kid ever. My little fluffy chunky Addison was sitting there just smiling and playing with her dolly. My son took her to the stairs and coached her as she crawled up. He would say, clapping his hands together, "Come on pooh dare you can make it, come on pooh dare." He couldn't say Pooh Bear! We called her Pooh Bear because a few weeks earlier we were at the grocery store and a lady thought she and my son looked like two fluffy bears! I've taught them both from a very young age to always take care of each other no matter what and be there for each other. I can truly say they have stood true to that even with a lot of sibling fights, but they still love each other. To build their character, let me tell you a few of their attributes.

We spent lots of days and evenings at the lake and park having picnics and watching the sunset. That was free! We'd go out to eat every Thursday night to "Pic A Dilly's" where I'd teach them

125

Airyka Edwards

to choose and order their own food. I also would teach them proper etiquette when at home or at a restaurant. My kids were inseparable. As they grew older, Addison looked to her brother for everything.

From about nine months old until adulthood my daughter would have frequent nose bleeds. Every time she had one during the night she would never wake me, she always went to her brother. He would clean her up, change her sheets and he'd go quietly back to bed after tucking her back in. Almost every time she'd end up sneaking back into her brothers room and fall asleep, lying her head on his back. What a sweet sight to see!

I taught my children to give and always share with the less fortunate, not that we had anything more. I remember our second Christmas together in our house. My son loved his Ninja Turtle figurines, even some he never took out of the box. Every Christmas I collected can goods and other nonperishable's for the local shelter in our town. My job would allow me to order extra turkeys when I gave dietary the number for my employees. I was allowed three to five extra turkeys. With everything I collected at the nursing home I would load it up and Wisk it off to the shelter. I was always so happy when I would do that. I felt someone was going to have a nice holiday.

One year the shelter leaders gave me a name for a family who was in need. It was a young single mother and her ten year old son who had terminal cancer. I only had a few extra dollars myself but I went and bought a few extra toys for this family. When my son got wind of what it was for, I remember him going in his room and gathering every Ninja Turtle still intact. He packed them in a gift bag and said, "Mommy please give these to the little boy. I want to be a part of their Christmas." I said, with tears in my eyes, "But son, those are your favorite turtles." He said, "But Mom I'll get more some other time, but he needs these toys now, he might die." He asked if he and his sister could meet the family. I wasn't too fond of strangers meeting my children, but I agreed. It was a Hispanic family on the other side of town. It was a Christmas I'll never forget, so rewarding, so touching. I told my son he did exactly what God wanted him to do at Christmas time because that's what it's all about!

Two weeks later we heard of a house fire, Terry, my buddy, at work (maintenance director) asked if we could once again help a family in need. This time my little Addison had the opportunity to give. A little girl around her age and size had lost all of her items in the fire. Addison packed her favorite house coat, which was her only house coat, pajamas, and two baby dolls to donate. My children had inherited my giving heart. All I can do was cry and thank God I had them. They are like that still today! Brett and his girls came into our lives. The five children were very close and truly loved each other. They continue to stay in touch with each other.

When we PCS'ed to Germany, my daughter wanted to stay involved with different activities; such as cheerleading and ballet. They both loved the youth center. I remember one Friday night the youth center had a dance where we could pay and drop them off until 10 P.M. My son couldn't wait to tell me that his sister was breaking it down on the dance floor! My son was on the shy side, always in the corner, but observing all the festivities. He was involved with soccer, baseball and flag football. He also loved to

Airyka Edwards

bowl. He was in the news paper on weekly basis in Texas for being on the five to seven year old league and had high points in every game!

In baseball the coach could not believe the pitch that kid had! They loved him. In soccer he was just as good. Once in Germany it was so cold during one of the games and his asthma was flaring up that week pretty bad! But he wanted to play. Brett always taught them if you start it, don't quit. Quitting wasn't an option, he had to finish, but Brett was deployed at the time. My son loved the game. I got to the game late after getting off work. I saw him having a rough time, running during the game, so I ran to the gate to hand him his inhaler. He looked at me and beckoned me to go back to the bleachers and let him play. He yelled, "I'm fine Mom. Go back!" I did as he asked.

My son was diagnosed with chronic asthma around nine to twelve months old. We made frequent trips to the emergency room, at 2 A.M. He simply couldn't breathe. Some nights he'd come in my room when he was two or three years old around, 1 to 2 A.M. saying, "Mommy please get up and take me to the doctor I can't breathe. I'm having another asthma attack!" Knowing I had to be at work by 7 A.M., I would drag myself out of bed to take him. My daughter had a chronic illness also "ear infections", so weeks after just settling down with one child I had to take Addison in to see her primary doctor. He said she needed tubes in her ears.

As the saying goes, "When it rains it pours." It felt like it had started to snow on me! Two weeks later, she was in surgery. I remember asking them to let her wear her red nightgown in

128

No Longer Bound

surgery, because her little thighs were so chunky and she looked adorable in it! We made it through that trimester.

Back in Germany, they tried keeping busy with as much as they could. We PCS'd to Louisiana, where my son played football in seventh and eighth grades while our daughter did flag line, band and Cheer. On a bittersweet happy note, my son's football game was the first game I'd ever gone to! (Laugh) My mother would tell me when I'd ask her if I could go to our school games, "Yes sweetheart you can go...if it's in the back yard!" So needless to say I was thirty six years old screaming at the games not knowing if it was a touchdown or mishap! A couple times my husband had to tell me to hush, as I screaming for the other team! My blonde roots would often come out!

The children finally hit high school and our son started to date a little. He went to his first prom and homecoming by sophomore and junior years. Brett was so proud to help him with his tie. It sounds simple but we enjoyed being a part of the kids' lives before they started to push us off.

Our daughter went to her first homecoming dance. Brett bought her a beautiful dress! She had an extra visitor going to homecoming with her, me! She was one mad little girl, but she got over it. My children were model children in school. I rarely ever got a call or note home for any type of behavior problems. Throughout the school each year, every teacher at every school my children attended knew my name because I was a concerned mom and an involved mother. I helped with homework, went to every single PTO meeting and attended any event my children ever had. Not to discredit my mother, but I wished so many days

Airyka Edwards

she would have just pretended to care enough to attend just one teachers meeting when I was in school. I always knew I would be hands on mom and I enjoyed every bit of it!

Addison was heavily into dance, tap, ballet, modeling and pageants. She was traveling with the competition dance team from "The School of Performing Arts", traveling to Florida, Oklahoma, Branson, Missouri and so many other places. She modeled for ETC Bridal. She also was in an associate program for college while in high school to obtain her Associates Degree in early Childhood Development. She graduated with nineteen college credits, the girl just soared! She was my little go team go girl! She was good at everything she had going and we were so proud of her! The pageants she was participating in just showed her radiance! People loved to be around her. She was witty and just a fun outgoing personality; although she had a mean streak that could be seen at times if people agitated her.

By age seventeen she graduated from high school, already was in college and dating. I'd just come home from two weeks of traveling for work having arrived home around 4 P.M. As I stated in Part 1 our daughter became pregnant. She called me around 2 A.M. to inform me she had gone into labor. I rushed over to pick her up and took her to the base hospital. By 10 A.M. she was taken by helicopter to the university hospital in another town. Her father and I drove like mad men to reach her. We finally reached the hospital after a couple hours, rushed to her room to find her with two to three doctors and tons of nurses, one of whom was holding her lifeless child. The baby had taken one breath and stopped breathing. All I could think is we missed holding her hand

130

No Longer Bound

and being there for her as we had always been. By age twenty she'd moved in and out with roommates around ten times!

That was just the beginning of the dark, crooked path that lies ahead for her! Her child passed away once the heart stopped beating completely. Shortly before all the final commotion the chaplain pressured us about naming and baptizing our grandson. We had not prepared for any of this because around twenty weeks into my daughter's pregnancy she came to visit me at work one day. My friend asked, "So has he started to kick or move yet?" Addison replied, "Uhmm, no I haven't felt any kicking or moving." Jenny and I looked at each other with a panic without trying to upset Addison. We put her on a table in a room. We grabbed a Doppler and listened for FHT (fetal heart tones) and we heard it. We both thought why aren't you feeling kicking, but Addison didn't have a clue. She went to her appointment the following Thursday to face bad news. She was told her child had not and would not fully develop lungs. She called me from her doctor's office because she didn't understand all the fancy medical terminology the OB doctor was telling her. She said, "Please call my mom. She was an OB clinic nurse and she'll understand."

The doctor sadly told me that her child had Pulmonary Hypoplasia and Absent Amniotic Fluid. I felt really bad for Addison, because I was so distant during her pregnancy due to disappointment and also because I knew she had to carry this child full term with the knowledge it was going to die shortly after birth. So for thirty two weeks she had to keep this child inside her merely to allow him to pass away on his own.

Airyka Edwards

We fought with the chaplain and nurse because Addison, her dad and I talked about trying to do an easy transition of separation by not naming the child or doing anything that would require attachment. But minutes later I had to help my child make the decision to move forward. She was so out of it from the medication they'd given her on the way and during childbirth. Minutes later her boyfriend showed up, he and I had words earlier as Brett and I were driving to the hospital. The child's father was allegedly intoxicated he couldn't help her.

Weeks before I was on the phone with my daughter. She was so sad over the choices she had made as her boyfriend was busy yelling at her in the background. Sadly he was fighting his own demons. I really wanted to rescue her, but at the same time I wanted her to feel a fraction of the hell she was putting us through. When it was all said and done, we stuck by her regardless of her choices! Her father sat there by her bedside, holding her hand as I lay on the couch in her hospital room. I was so tired after arriving from Kentucky from two weeks of working different shifts and not getting proper sleep I could hardly function. I remember waking up and Brett was walking her to the bathroom to help her clean up. He stood by the door and waited on her to help her back into bed. Then I heard her say her favorite words, "Dad, I'm hungry." That's when I knew she was okay. (Laugh)

We took our daughter home once again to take care of her and nurse her back to good health. We had her child baptized, named and cremated. I'm a little jealous he made it to heaven before me!

Addison moved on, getting a job full time. She saved enough money for a car. She called me one morning in February 2011 to say she would be over. She had moved again with friends. That cold February evening she came over to tell me she needed help because she had started using meth! I simply said, "Okay I guess I should help since you asked." She stated she did not want to get to the point of no return. So again the next morning I got up went to work, did my job as usual and told my director I needed off the next day to take my child to rehab a few hours away where I found a place that could accept her. My boss looked at me and said, "My goodness, how did you make it through the day with all of this on your mind?" I simply said, "I had a job to do and I had to stay focused and pray."

So off she went for a few weeks then she cried to come home. I fell for it and went to pick her up; it just so happened I had to work in that town that day. It wasn't long after that she was living with us again. One night as her father and I were watching TV in our room I heard her getting dressed. She came in to say "I'll be back shortly I'm going out with friends." I looked directly in her eyes and said, "Addison you shouldn't leave the house tonight." "But Mom," she said, "Seriously, don't start. I'll be back." I said, "Okay Addy you've been warned." She smirked and said, "Oooh weee, are we having another premonition?" I just looked at her and laid back down.

We went to sleep around 9:30 P.M. that night. I remember the phone ringing about 11 P.M., I hurriedly answered, the voice on the other end asked, "Ma'am may I speak to Airyka Edwards?" I stated, "She is speaking, sir." "Ma'am this is the Ambulance Department we have your daughter, she's been in a motor vehicle accident." I didn't get excited. I asked, "Is she okay?" "Well, ma'am, she rolled over in a truck with some friends. She wasn't driving, but no seat

Airyka Edwards

belt and they all had been drinking. We're transporting her to the hospital." I said, "Okay tell her to call when she's discharged!" I turned over, Brett asked, "Dear is everything okay?" I said, "Yes honey, it's Addy, she's ok."

By January 2012 she wanted to get out of town, so she moved about an hour away. She said, "Maybe I need to change friends and scenery." It doesn't matter where you run if you're troubled, it will find you.

On the rebound from a bad breakup with her boyfriend she was to marry, who had allegedly cheated on her, she was ready for war and the world. She seemed to be really trying to make it. Brett stated one day, "So dear we really should try and help our daughter a little." I was opposed by now because she moved here, there and everywhere and back again, I was done with that part of her life.

We had some extra money from Brett selling an old jeep we had that I'd threatened to burn if he didn't get rid of it! So with that money he put five hundred dollars down on a car for Addison and sent my stepdaughter the rest for her upcoming wedding. We took her car filled it with gas, brought groceries for her and her roommate; we helped them fix their place up somewhat and then headed home. I noticed around Easter that year she didn't act like my "normal" Addison.

By July she wasn't coming home as she had previous weekends. It was approaching my dad's birthday July twenty-seventh so I was honestly looking for a distraction, but not the one God planned for me that day! My husband was on the phone ordering one of

134

his girls a floral gift basket for her birthday on the twenty-ninth. We were upstairs. I rarely check my cell phone on weekends, because people know to call me on my house phone. Just so happen around noon I went downstairs to get water for Brett and I stopped to check my cell. Oh my! I have five missed calls from her friend Theresa. I thought "Huh I wonder why she didn't call the home phone?" Therese and her family were close friends. I called her back to hear in her frantic voice, "Mrs. Airyka, Addison was taken by ambulance to the hospital!" I asked Therese to calm down and I asked what was going on now. She yelled, "I don't know Mrs. Airyka, but it's bad!" So I hung up my cell phone and called the hospital. The operator Lisa answered and I calmly asked, "Hey lady this is Airyka, someone called and said my daughter is in the emergency room. Lisa can you please go check and see what's going on?" She said, "Yes girl hold on." I held and when she returned to the phone she said, "Airyka Edwards, just get up here now!! I mean now!" I told Brett to watch Maddison and her friend; I had to run up to the hospital Addy was there. I left my truck out front and ran in the hospital. They never asked, the girls just pushed the doors opened and buzzed me through! My pageant queen, my pooh bear was lying there lifeless. I saw machines hooked up to my child that are only used for people that can't breathe on their own! My child was on life support! The doctor came in as I went into shock seeing her like that! I knew the physician who was taking care of her, Dr. Deckard an awesome physician and a, sweet man! He began to tell me what they'd done so far trying to save her. He asked if I wanted her transferred to our larger sister facility in the next town over about an hour away. I hurriedly replied, "No!" I said, "Dr. Deckard, I've worked ER with you before." He said, "I know, I remember." He said, "Okay, we

Airyka Edwards

are going to take great care of her." I had no doubt about the care at our hospital, I worked there. I knew what kind of care we give.

Before long RT (Respiratory Therapy) was ordered, to manage her breathing while on the ventilator, nuclear med was ordered for MRI and so many other things were going on. I stood by her bedside looking at my baby girl and I'm beating myself up, wondering what happened to get her there not just that day but to get her here in life.

As I was standing there holding my child's cold brittle hand, coworkers who knew me started to come into the room, from nuclear med. They asked if I wanted to call Brett to let him know what was going on, but by now I didn't know if hours or just minutes had passed. I told them, "I'm sorry I can't think. I don't know my number at home!" Brenda, one of Addison's past ballet buddies took my phone to look up my number. Cheyenne and Lisa stayed with me for hours. They said, "Airyka, let's pray." For the first time in my life I couldn't. They said, "Never mind, it's okay. We'll pray with you, and for your daughter." I stood there and just cried. My heart was hurting so bad and no one but God could help me. I literally felt like three elephants were sitting on my chest. I had so many coworkers at my side ready and waiting for anything I needed. I didn't need anything. I just wanted my child back in one piece, smiling and saying she was hungry.

The doctor came back in and kept checking on my daughter and me. They moved her to ICU (Intensive Care Unit). They had to unplug her ventilator to move her bed down the hall, so they manually bagged her breathing. She had IV's and tubing everywhere.

No Longer Bound

Honestly I can't exactly remember when Brett arrived at the hospital, but I knew when he got there I had left her room to sit out in the ICU waiting area. I just needed to breathe. I forgot I hadn't notified any of my family, not even my son! I texted my sister in Texas and asked for prayer; I don't remember if I got a response. I texted my boss; I believe it was around 7 P.M. not real sure. They dropped everything to come be with Brett and me. Bless their hearts! They had been floating on the river all day. They assumed we were at the larger hospital in the town over and they drove there to find we were at our hospital where we worked. Thomas, Ranae, and Dallas were there for us all the way. I would receive prayers, Bible scriptures and words of encouragement daily from Dallas who was only eighteen years old, but wise for his age.

As I sat in the ICU waiting area, I looked through my phone; I'd received at least fifty text messages. I happen to glance at the date; it was my dad's birthday, July 27th. I was too numb to cry any more. I held my head in my hands and said, "God please, please don't do this to me on my dad's birthday. God, I can handle a lot of things, but I can't do this one, Lord. I ask you, God, please take this cup from me!"

I recall once again talking to my dad. I asked him to watch over my daughter and wake her up. I was desperate. Soon Brett had to leave and wanted me to go home. He could tell I was not just exhausted, but mentally collapsing fast! But a mother always seems to find strength. I told him to go take care of our grandchild, because there was no way I was leaving my daughter's side. As the night moved on, the hospital quieted some. Visiting hours were over, but this was my resident until my baby woke up. They

137

Airyka Edwards

fixed a chair for me with many warm blankets, but I didn't need any of that. I don't recall closing my eyes, only long enough to simply blink! I stood most of the night by her bed still holding her ice cold hand. The nurses along with "RT" came in several times during the night to try and wean her off the ventilator. Every attempt failed. She could not breathe on her own. One nurse I hadn't seen in years was my daughters nurse that night said, "Well Airyka, all we can do is wait to see if she makes it through the night." What mother wants to hear that? She said, "Honey, you know we are going to do everything we can." I had no doubt.

Over the next few days my coworkers at the hospital carefully checked on me and constantly reminded me, "Airyka, we're here, all you have to do is say what you need." My coworkers in eight years had never seen me without a smile no matter what I had gone through. They knew this was not something I could bare. The next day came and her friends wanted to flood the hospital. I made a request that no one was allowed near my child, no visitors, no calls, not even a flower. The nurses and other staff respected our wishes. However Theresa's parents, Molly and Reggie came to visit as we have all been friends for years.

By the third day God saw fit to wake my baby up and breath the breathe of life into her once more! But now she had another problem that was discovered during x-rays and MRI. She had a bad gallbladder! The very next day they prepped her for a "Cholecystectomy" which is commonly called a "Lapchole". She was blessed to make it through surgery and by mid week she was discharged.

No Longer Bound

She wondered, "Mom what am I going to do? I don't have anywhere to go?" She didn't have a clue we had already moved her belongings back home. We informed her and she was thrilled! We moved her back with the condition she had to go off to rehab. She cried, "Mom and Dad please don't send me off. I'll be fine if you guys just help me." I was adamant. We gave her two weeks to recover from surgery and when she was cleared we took her three hours away where none of her friends could find her. She was gone for about a month. She attended a few church services while there. She told us that for the first time in years she realized if she had died she would have gone to hell! I asked, "How do you know that?" She said, "Mom I purposely allowed what happened to me and I wouldn't have been able to ask forgiveness." She said, "That's suicide." I was amazed!

My children were brought up in the Pentecostal faith. They knew very well what I stood for and believed. My son has always been a God-fearing believer but my Addison was not so sure God even existed. They were introduced to God not religion. I've always tried to encourage, but not force religion on my children. God began to work with her. She came back with a woman's devotional Bible and actually read it daily.

After she return home, we explained to her we would help her with a healthy transition back into the "normal work world" in a few months, but during the time with us she was not allowed any visitors or calls. She did really well and November came she was so excited about going to Texas with us to visit friends. Two days before we were to leave, she said she wanted her nails done and to go look for a job so that when we returned she could go to work. We didn't see any harm in that. I'd told a friend mine, about

Airyka Edwards

a month prior I saw "an itch, she's getting anxious about leaving the house and it is getting harder to hold her in".

We took her shopping to buy new clothes. She loved making roped necklaces with pendants, so we bought tons of materials for her to stay busy. She sold her necklaces for ten dollars and made one hundred dollars in one day just at my job. She is such a talented young lady, but when the drugs called she answered!

It was Tuesday night she was supposed to be home by 7 P.M. and she was late. I called and she made excuses. I said, "Come home now or never come back!" She was there in thirty minutes or so. She was high again! The hurt and disappointment, I could never explain the bitter pill I had to swallow that night. She said, "I know the rules. I just came to get my clothes." My husband came downstairs hearing the commotion. I asked her, "Please just tell me why? Why? What did we do to make you run back out and do this to us or to yourself? For God's sake, you died and God gave you another chance, not a second chance but another chance!" I was beside myself. I ran outside to the young ladies car that she was riding with. I wanted to rip her out of that car and beat her to a pulp for helping my daughter do this! Although in reality that little girl didn't twist my daughters arm, she was just a ride, that young lady was so out of it it wasn't funny! She couldn't have told you her name.

Brett came out to pull me back in but I was a raging lunatic that night. Brett finally got me back in the house and I couldn't think straight so I let the anger go. I began to plead with Addison, "Please just go upstairs and sleep it off. I'll over look one mistake." "No" she said, "you told me zero tolerance for drugs." I cried,

140

No Longer Bound

"You have come too far for me to give up on you now." I got on my knees crying, "Please please don't do this to me!" I begged and she turned around and asked me, "Do you like my nails Mom?" I was, "Oh my! I'm pleading and you want to know if I like your nails!" I turned around and went upstairs; she left out.

Brett locked the door, came upstairs and held me in his arms. I cried so hard. He tried to comfort me. He's never been good in situations like that, but that night he was my rock! I cannot explain the pain, hurt, anger and numbness once again. I felt like a failure!

We got up the next morning and drove to Texas for Thanksgiving to visit my friend. (We had a wonderful visit!) I had several calls from Addison begging us to turn around and come get her. She's sorry and she wants to be with her family. We were an hour or two away, Brett asked, "Dear do you want to turn around?" I stuck to my guns. I said, "No! She's hurt us all." She kept calling and finally I told her how I felt. I believe that was the first time I actually vented to her about how I really felt. I've always tried to let my children know if I was disappointed, unhappy or whatever, but always in a kind way. If I was proud of them I voiced that also. I learned early on to praise children before constructive criticism. They always received it pretty well. That morning I told her in a dissatisfying voice how upset and hurt I was. Once again we were left with a baffled thought "WHY"?

Brett told me to stop saying the things I was saying to her that morning; I held nothing back. He said he was so afraid of her committing suicide after I voiced my bruised crushed feelings! I was so tired of the repeated effortless attempts to try and rehabilitate Addison. This was the first Thanksgiving without my

Airyka Edwards

daughter. During this same time frame yours truly was not only dealing with our daughter, but my son had his demons being active at the same time! Yes double whammy for me and mine!

It was finally approaching Christmas and I wanted to do a little shopping. Addison called one Saturday and wanted to ride with us, so again we allowed her to tag along. We noticed certain stores she would not go in with us, but we didn't think odd about that, because there have been many occasions she didn't like the store we shopped at. I noticed when we got home that evening Addison had a look on her face as if she stolen a piece of cake..... well I wish it had been a piece of cake! She confessed that while out getting high she and her girlfriend during that Thanksgiving episode she had gone to a certain store and stole an item and got caught. It turned out over the next few months that she had a string of theft charges and traffic tickets. I refused to help with any of her legal problems.

One night a few weeks later, she called to talk to me. She said it was important. After I got home from work she came over. We sat down and I gave her my undivided attention. She proceeds to tell me she has "cancer"! I said, "Cancer?" "Yes ma'am Cancer", when did you find out?" She said, "I've known for a week now but didn't want to worry you. Well I have to go, but before I go can you loan me some money to pay a couple of tickets? I have court tomorrow and if I don't pay I go to jail." I said, "No ma'am the money tree has run out and I guess you'll just have to go jail." Sadly I worked with the city officials in Wellness and of course they all knew me and by now they all knew my children too! My children just continued to oblige their craving for lies, sins and drugs. They continue to

No Longer Bound

destroy their lives. I got to the point of breakage and weakness. I reached out to God one night like I never had before!

While in Louisiana, My son was in trouble once for being with a group of boys he shouldn't have been. That was his first bout with trouble around age fourteen; at this time I started to see his sky turning grey. My son's life has been just as troubled as my daughter's. He has always been an observer not a leader. Once he has set his eyes on his prey however then he launches for it! He evolved from this sweet innocent creature over to a young hardened adult. I could never understand why and how he became so hardened, because life wasn't bad for either of my children growing up. I think as soon as he realized just how the world worked, he quickly shifted into low gear. His ultimate goal was to have what the other guys on the corner had, but I don't think he thought about the conquences and the responsibilities that came with the job. His life very quickly went from bright yellow warm and fuzzy to grim, straight into darkness! It all came to an abrupt end one day in another town with one of his closest friends. He was busted for drugs! He was in a relationship with my second grandchild's mother. They had a wonderful relationship for a couple of years before it started to go sour. My son was hot tempered and very unfaithful to one I'll call "Summer" to reserve her privacy.

Summer was a very hardworking young lady, and well educated. She has a degree in education and a degree in cosmetology, which she utilizes today. She's a well liked person from an awesome home, with wonderful parents, Martha & Kurt. Inside and out she is gorgeous, but beauty and brains weren't enough to hold my son's interest down. He was thirsty for more of everything. When he was stable and focused, working hard every night, he managed to purchase himself a very nice new car. He had a nice nest egg saved and life was great until the dark began to look bright green to him. He struggled with his demons daily.

Material gain (things) has never held my son's attention. I asked him one day, "Son what makes you happy? What is it in life that can make you jump for joy and run down the street because happiness has you?" He thought about it, but didn't have to think long. He said, "Mom, "really" there's nothing that trips my trigger as far as happiness. I don't really know what I'm after in life." I realize the devil doesn't care what you want; he will give you something (a taste) and make you crave more. My mother would say, "You can drive a horse to water, but you can't make 'em drink it."

We had allowed our son to move back home on several occasions trying to help him get ahead and off the streets. The outcome, however is that he doesn't "drink the water". He is and has been one of the sweetest kids I've met in my lifetime. He hates to see little children being mistreated. He has always said yes, ma'am, no sir, yes sir to whomever, even hold the door open for his elders, but yet he didn't love his own children enough to work and take care of them. They deserved stability and he didn't give them that. I deserve to lie down at night and know my child is safe and secure in life, but I didn't get that either.

I remember being so angry with him at his first born's first birthday party. We gave a party fit for a sixteen year old princess. A lot of her mother's family came. I knew my son was traveling from out of state so I prolonged the candle blowing until he got there, thirty minutes passed, an hour, hour and a half, finally I had to go ahead as the crowd was growing anxious. He makes it back to Missouri safely about the gift opening time. She had tables full of gifts! He walked in, I was so happy to see him until I looked in his eyes. He apparently was high but not seriously impaired. I was appalled! Embarrassed doesn't even touch the surface of what I felt, but I had to put my happy face on as I had always done for years in front of other people.

He and the mother participated in the rest of the events for their daughter. Afterwards we gathered everything, while our granddaughter stayed the night with her "Mimi", another person our little one bonded with at birth. Those two together are inseparable!

I told my son not to come to the house until he was straight. I was so disappointed that he only thought of himself. He used the lame excuse, "Mom, I was just so nervous about all those people there, I stated that was not acceptable."

He continually drove a wedge between Summer and I just so I'd always stay on his side. A couple of years ago I met up with her to pick up my granddaughter. My son didn't bank on us chatting for about an hour that day. So many instances where he lied to us both about his rent. She would help him "already being a single parent" with no child support. I was helping also. She nicely asked if I could help him with his last month's rent in his apartment. I stated, "No! I've helped him for months." She stated, "Well, he said you never had the money to help." The web of lies began to unfold, he told to the two women who loved him the most. As that old saying goes, "never bite the hand that feeds you." He did, with lie after lie, but God was looking out for us both. His

Airyka Edwards

money train was over! His deception was despicable! I was so hurt, wounded and injured.

Drugs, evil and greed doesn't have a face or a title, but even then God gave me the strength to forgive him and be more aware. I prayed that God would give Summer the will and strength to let my son go. God answered that prayer. That was a hard prayer for two people I so loved, but she certainly deserved someone better than my son. I'm so grateful God gave us a stronger relationship and we learned. We still love my son, but we know now "not" to allow him to manipulate us anymore.

I've told both of my children I never thought I'd see the day I had to talk with them behind bars! God helped me and answered my prayer. I didn't cry anymore, nor sob myself to sleep, nor leave large sums of money on their account in jail. From what I hear commissary is really expensive in jail. I was not going to make them comfortable. My son has had his share of hard knocks, but mostly self induced. I pray for them each and every night. If they call "Mom, I'm hungry." I can nicely say, "Well honey I'll pray for you and I love you." They've used that line often because I've always said, "I'll never let you go hungry." No money of mine will reach their hands again. Life is short for some and long for others, then we die. I've had to forgive them an awful lot in the last few years for the lies, the disappointments and simply just for going astray, but that is what Moms and Dads do.

Now even as I celebrate my dad's birthday each year I don't dwell on my sadness, yes I think of him often, but looked to God for strength and healing. This year I was busy being a blessing to someone who was thirteen years old. I was able to share my

No Longer Bound

testimony concerning my struggles, "as she" struggles with Bulimia and Anorexia. Let's just say, "Healing has begun!"

If you can relate to any of my heartaches concerning my children, just let them go, stop fighting. It's their battle with the devil and their demons. Your job is just like mine, pray for them daily that God is allowed to take control of their lives. I hope I've given you strength to continue and maintain. Remember the battle never ends, but the fight does! Be encouraged!

"..........the race is not to the swift; nor the battle to the strong....." Ecclesiastes 9:11 KJV

"My Christmas Prayer"......I cried out "God please give me the strength to make it through the holidays. Lord please, allow my children to make it through the holidays!" I said, "Lord, if you grant me that, things are going to change after the first of the year. Lord, I will make you a promise and keep it. God, I humbly ask for "strength just through the holidays" and from henceforth Lord, I'm yours, my mind is yours. I rededicate my life totally to you with no distractions and I will give you my children back. God, I'm sorry for holding on to them from the start. I would not have had to bear such needless pain. All that I am, all that I think, all that I see, all that I speak, everywhere I go I give it all to you. Everything I do, God, I give it all to you.

When you can't fix it, let it go and let God!

Chapter Thirteen

Our Transition To "Missouri" Part II

My New Year's Resolution

I'm Going To Rehab!

I Have Been Set Free!

As you read in my Christmas prayer I asked God to help me through the holidays. At Christmas I tried to make it my goal from the time my children and I started off together, to always make our holidays joyous, with or without anyone else. When I reached that abrupt stage in my life when joy and happiness no longer existed for me, because of my children's behavior I had to totally rely on my God and my faith.

I'd gone to my doctor to see medically what was going on. I'd started losing large amounts of hair, no appetite and I started getting seriously depressed. My doctor asked me a few questions and did some blood work. We sat and talked for over an hour. I kind of felt bad since there were other patients waiting to see him, but I had to remember "even the nurse's need nursing". My doctor said my diagnosis was stress. My stress levels were so

No Longer Bound

high that it caused the hair loss. My marriage was soaring, doing better than ever. My doctor, also being a close friend asked me to be truthful, so I started to tell him what I had gone through in the last few months. He said, "I do truly understand." I backed him up saying, "No, no you don't and you can't unless you have been there." He sat talking and crossed his arms with a puzzled look on his face and said, "Airyka, sweetie, I do know, because I live with it! My child is an addict too. It is so bad I have to sleep with my bedroom door locked, just to protect my wife and I." Wow, I was taken back. I apologized for the assumption. I know drugs have no face, no culture.

I was still going to church as usual and one Saturday Brett asked, "Are you going to church tomorrow?" I said, "Yes, why?" He said, "Well sweetheart that is a lot of gas you burn going back and forth like that." I looked at him and said, "Honey, right now my church and my faith is my sanity, that's all I have." He apologized and said, "Dear I'm sorry I know the kids are putting you through a rough time, go as much as you like."

God helped me through those dark days during the holidays. One day shortly after New Year's Brett was in his office at home doing paperwork. I was visiting with him sitting there just talking. I told him I'll be back later. "Where are you going?" he asked, "I'm going over to Memorial Funeral Home. He stopped typing and turned around in his chair and said, "May I ask why? You hate funeral homes." I said, "I know I'm going to make arrangements for the kids." "Dear did something happen I don't know about." Brett said. I said with a smile, "No nothing happened yet, but if it does I want to be prepared. Why should I leave all of the arrangements to you, because I would not be in any condition to take care of

149

Airyka Edwards

anything like that! I probably would get mad later if you had to make arrangements and you didn't do something right. I figured if the children are going to kill themselves I might as well be prepared and besides that, God has released and delivered me from them." I gave my children over to God which I should have done years ago way before now, so off to the funeral home I went!

One thing about a place like that it never closes! Maddison and I drove over. I asked the receptionist for Mrs. Shelly Wright she said, "Sweetie she's busy right now in her office." I said, "Ma'am just tell her Airyka Edwards from the hospital is here to see her." Shelly heard that and jumped out of her seat and came to the front lobby where I was "as Maddison collected mints and Kleenex's" [Laugh]

She grabbed my hand with this frantic look, "Airyka, sweetheart is everything okay?" I smiled and said, "Yes ma'am everything's fine." "I don't understand Airyka Edwards, then what's going on." I explained, "Mrs. Shelly my children have been into things that has potential of taking their lives." I explained to her a few months back with Addison's ordeal and is now back out there on the prowl. My son had guys looking for him to the extent he called me to ask, "Mom please tell me what I should do." I said, "Son, if you have never listened to me before, listen now, come home like now and I mean in the next few minutes. When we hang up, get out of your apartment." I told him I didn't care if he brought clothes or not. So he did, hours later as soon as darkness hit a neighbor called him to let him know about five or six guys were kicking his door down! Thanks be to God! My son was safe at home in another town. I said, "Mrs. Shelly, Brett and I talked

150

No Longer Bound

to him. We offered to move him back home the following week when things calmed down, but instead my son thought he had something to prove. So back to his place he went. Another guy he said was on his back because my son said he backed into his car. They agreed to settle with a handshake and cash in about a week. My son didn't have the money; he'd just lost his job after a few years of working. So Mama comes to the rescue and wires him one hundred fifty dollars, then the next month it was I'm short on rent and so on. I told her God showed me clearly I cannot help my son; there wasn't any amount of money I can give him to settle him down; there were no fancy words to ease him, so God released me from my son.

Weeks later Addison told me she had cancer, when she knew that was another ploy for more money, then she jumped out in front of a truck to purposely get hit. She played the part well to get drugs, but no insurance money. Sorry about her luck!

Earlier that week I had to call one of my patients to tell him he really did have cancer! He was shocked and was worried about his wife. I assured him I would guide him through his treatments and be there every step of the way for him and his wife. While my daughter lies about such a thing and there are real people suffering and dying from cancer!

So Mrs. Shelly and I ended our chat with her giving me the papers I needed to fill out and bring back to her. To my amazement my husband filled his out also. I however didn't know he wanted to be cremated; he does not want to be buried. I would advise everyone to do a "Will and Living Will", make your own decisions.

Airyka Edwards

I took Mrs. Shelly the pamphlets back all filled out for my family, namely my children and stated that they would be cremated, because if I survive them I want to take my children with me should I move since I am not from here.

I also informed my kids that they were going to be cremated. They both were livid stating, "We don't want to be cremated!" I nicely informed them, "I don't get the choice to keep you alive and well so you don't get the choice on how you're put away!" I actually got a little pleasure out of seeing them seriously upset!

My eight year span of worrying about them, losing hair and sleep was over! God held up his end, I had asked him to take us all through the holidays, so I held up to mine! I am "No longer bound" or conformed to my children! You don't know how good that feels unless you walk or have walked in those shoes. It's been so peaceful letting someone else worry with my children, "their maker". So hear me when I say "I have been rehabbed!" I was an addict for my children; as the rehab prayer/ acknowledgement go: One: you admit you are "powerless", that your life had been unmanageable. Two: I came to believe that a "Power" greater than mine could restore me back to "sanity". I told you, my readers, you "can" regain or gain your sanity.

I have been set free! My children can no longer manipulate me! If they wish to continue with their life styles so be it! I have given all I have to try to make a better life for them. My children have told us many times "I'm grown, you can't keep telling us what to do and treating us like kids." My thoughts now, "Thank you for releasing me of Mommy duties!"

No Longer Bound

I pray every single day for my children, several times a day, but I'm no longer overcome by grief from midnight calls, because something is after them or because they've had some drug to make them hallucinate. It's not just Missouri, drugs are everywhere. Missouri didn't do any of this to my children; it was the choices they made. I had to read a book to learn about illegal drugs. There is an awesome book called Ozark Meth by Laura Valenti. That drug alone with heroin is like candy here. I will continue to pray for all those out there that is or has dealt with a similar situation. My life is all about my God, my faith and my walk with him. We can't fix a person, that doesn't want to be fixed. I could not be rehabilitated until I acknowledged that there was a problem and I was powerless over it! I'm thankful to God that "I went to Him!" I have been REHABED! I have been Set Free!

Chapter Fourteen

My Purpose

To Inform & To Encourage

I sincerely hope that you have been blessed and inspired with my hardships and my triumphs. God knew he would take me on this journey to bring me full circle today. I'm grateful and so appreciative of all the experiences God allowed me to encounter. So many occasions I had to "laugh through the pain" to make it through the day, my laughter often brightens another's day. It would help me cover my hurt. I knew that one day in due season that if I endured "my joy cometh in the morning". It's hard to foresee the joy when you are being overcome by years of excruciating pain day after day. Even though I know my purpose is being a healer I personally had to be responsible for my own healing. It may sound cruel to have to heal yourself, but know this: when the healer is taking care and cleaning the wound of another as you praise, as you encourage, as you put the bandage on another person's hurt you begin to believe for them. You begin to listen to yourself. The healer always gets comfort and has pride as the end result. You feel like a champ when you help someone else through their pain.

No Longer Bound

If I have to give an injection to one of my patients who is terrified of needles, my job is to make them feel comfortable and assure them I'm going to take good care of them. When I give my injection and they state, "Airyka, when are you going to give me my shot?" My response, "Sweetheart I'm finished already!" They are so grateful to you. I'm happy my patient is happy! Your healing comes through being a healer!

No matter what life throws at you. Learn how to turn your adversity into strength. I feel I was put on this earth to serve from a young age. I had to take on the form of a servant in order to survive. As God lead me through this process, I still searched to engage others in my metamorphosis. In this account I've taken you from my birth, through entering my teens, over into early adulthood, to land in my roles as mother, wife and total adulthood. It is that seed to flower, tadpole to frog and the chrysalis to butterfly.

My life went through the change of character and appearance to my transformation of now today! "Metamorphosis "I had a pronounced change in the form, from one stage to the next in my life; for you it can be, any complete change of form, structure, substance or circumstances, etc.

For that young lady or young man in the Projects that is thinking there's no way out, think twice! You already know how to survive, just use what you know. Go into survival mode and find your escape route and make your exit!

For the single young lady or man that seeks and yearns for a saved, smart, intelligent, educated young man or women; apply yourself by becoming smart, intelligent and educated, then reach for

155

excellence. Again I say, surround yourself with positive educated leaders in life. Give him what you want to receive. Excellence! Now see what God's got for you! "We" and that includes you, were made in his own image. Give Godliness and you'll receive a Godly man or woman!

For that person who is so despondent and discouraged, you feel profound hopelessness; hold your head up high! For as God said in,

John 14:27 KJV "Peace I leave with you; my peace I give you. Not as the world giveth, give I unto you. Let not your hearts be troubled neither let it be afraid."

Psalm 55:22 "Cast thy burdens upon the Lord, and he shall sustain thee, he shall never suffer the righteous to be moved." KJV

For all those who are struggling with addictions of all kinds, from any habitual sin, such as alcohol, substance abuse, pornography, Bulimia and Anorexia, cigarettes, other nicotine, what "EVER" it is, God's word said, "Therefore".

"Therefore if any man be in Christ he is a new creature old things have passed away; behold, all things are become new". II Corinthians 5:17 KJV

Jeremiah 29:11, KJV "For I know the thoughts that I think towards you, saith the Lord, thoughts of peace, and not evil (halleluiah)! To give you an expected end.

God has Plans to prosper you and not to harm you, plans to give you hope and a future".

So God's has plans for you! Please don't give up! Hold on, remember for in due season! *"....we shall reap if we faint not."* Galatians 6:9 KJV

I am reminded through the years as I continue to have my trials I have to stand; *"... Therefore my beloved brethren be ye steadfast, unmovable, always abounding in the work of the Lord, forasmuch as ye know that your labour is not in vain in the Lord."* I Corinthians 15:58 KJV

Sometimes we get discouraged along the way and may ask ourselves "Why do I continue"? "How do I know all that I do is not in vain?" The Clark Sisters sang a song, "Is my living in vain, is my praying in vain, am I wasting my time, can the clock be rewound?" They answered and said, "No! Of course not, it's not all in vain! But as for me, I don't care if there's no streets paved with gold in heaven, I just want to go! Until then I will continue to worship God at my church, namely because I love to hear Sister Janis yell out with her deep voice "Yesssssss Lord!" that lady's voice can make the angels stand at attention and praise God! When Brother Stewart gets this crazy look on his face and his head kind of turns to one side and he yells out, "I don't know what you came to do, but I came to "Praise my God!" About that time you hear our assistant Pastor, Elder Andrew say, "Come on Zion!" Shortly after that you can hear Brother Enock break out with a Doctor Watt note, but in today's version the praise and shouting is like a wild fire every time. If you look towards the left back pew you'll find Sister Airyka Edwards cutting her step! As the Holy Ghost keeps moving you'll see my pastor, break out of his seat and my sweet First Lady over to the right of the pulpit cutting hers, but it doesn't stop there, not before Elder Benny gets loose! I love the

Airyka Edwards

way my pastor is lead by God. There have been times I haven't said a word to him or anyone else, but my pastor, can sense and see the pain, the hurt in my eyes and soul. He allows God to manifest himself in him to help us. I thank God for my church and my church family. If you don't have a church home just find a "place in God" to help you through whatever it is you are going through.

I sincerely hope my biological sisters and brothers somehow find peace and their healing through some of my words. They went through things also, as we all tried to survive. I love them so dearly!

As I said earlier in another chapter this is merely an "edited" version of stages in my life. I will continue to live. I will continue to dream. Don't ever stop hoping and dreaming! I still hope that one day I can be a fifty and older fashion model or start a support group for "Bulimia and Anorexia". I also want to live in Texas and own a home, "beachfront" and wake up to the sound of waves with a cup of coffee in my hands! I'd also love to meet Ms. Oprah Winfrey and Ms. Ellen Degenres one day, but if none of this ever happens, I'd be happy continuing with my faith and sharing my life experiences trying to help someone through words of encouragement. I can truly say "I have gone through my own personal fire", but I'm proud to say.... "I am No Longer Bound".

As so many addictions have surrounded my family, I chose not to fall into cadence to our family curse of drugs, alcohol, gambling and poverty. I had a strong will; I have a strong faith in God, sometimes that's all I had. I had moments when I felt I had spiritual polio. I could still walk, but kept losing my balance. I needed

No Longer Bound

crutches, until deliverance came. I threw my crutches away. Just when I stood on my own two feet another disappointment came.

This year while visiting my family, my husband began to ask questions with my sister, my first cousin, my brother and brother-in-law. They were enjoying the evening inside the screened gazebo. My husband made a statement about the Indian tribe my mother was supposed to be a part of, mind you for fifty-one years I, along with other siblings, had been told by our mother that she was full Chickasaw Indian. Well, little to my dismay my sister was into genealogy. She found that our mother was NOT Chickasaw Indian, but rather our mother is an everyday average African American, "B-K" with a quarter of Indian in her! Because of her looks, we had no reason to question her. My husband tried to explain to me while heading back to the hotel that night with our daughter and granddaughters. I was so taken by the news I wouldn't even hear him out!

After arriving at the hotel I was in the bathroom changing and he tried talking again. I finally said, "I don't care! I don't want to know any of that. I just don't care." He walked out of the bathroom and said, "Dear, I'm sorry I was just trying to help." I felt really bad for not listening to him, but I was hurt, mad and totally outraged! Not because we weren't half Indian or because my mother wasn't, it was because another fabricated story, one I'd believed for fifty-one years, all of my life! I'd told my children that and they told their children!

I woke up early and went downstairs to get my morning fix, "coffee". I sat and did some thinking. Shortly after I returned to my room and apologized to my husband for my behavior. He

Airyka Edwards

accepted and said he knew the disappointment I felt, after all that storyline was the starting paragraph in my book!

Let's just say life is full of disappointments, heartaches and pains, but I'm not going to let that be an excuse to fall or stay down. I will continue to rise above the past and pain life brings, because when it's all said and done……

"It's My Voice and My Freedom"

"My Healing"

"I Am No Longer Bound"

Be Blessed!

To Be Continued